C-1024  CAREER EXAMINATION SERIES

*This is your*
*PASSBOOK for...*

# Senior Stationary Engineer

*Test Preparation Study Guide*
*Questions & Answers*

# COPYRIGHT NOTICE

This book is SOLELY intended for, is sold ONLY to, and its use is RESTRICTED to individual, bona fide applicants or candidates who qualify by virtue of having seriously filed applications for appropriate license, certificate, professional and/or promotional advancement, higher school matriculation, scholarship, or other legitimate requirements of education and/or governmental authorities.

This book is NOT intended for use, class instruction, tutoring, training, duplication, copying, reprinting, excerption, or adaptation, etc., by:

1) Other publishers
2) Proprietors and/or Instructors of "Coaching" and/or Preparatory Courses
3) Personnel and/or Training Divisions of commercial, industrial, and governmental organizations
4) Schools, colleges, or universities and/or their departments and staffs, including teachers and other personnel
5) Testing Agencies or Bureaus
6) Study groups which seek by the purchase of a single volume to copy and/or duplicate and/or adapt this material for use by the group as a whole without having purchased individual volumes for each of the members of the group
7) Et al.

Such persons would be in violation of appropriate Federal and State statutes.

PROVISION OF LICENSING AGREEMENTS – Recognized educational, commercial, industrial, and governmental institutions and organizations, and others legitimately engaged in educational pursuits, including training, testing, and measurement activities, may address request for a licensing agreement to the copyright owners, who will determine whether, and under what conditions, including fees and charges, the materials in this book may be used them.  In other words, a licensing facility exists for the legitimate use of the material in this book on other than an individual basis.  However, it is asseverated and affirmed here that the material in this book CANNOT be used without the receipt of the express permission of such a licensing agreement from the Publishers. Inquiries re licensing should be addressed to the company, attention rights and permissions department.

All rights reserved, including the right of reproduction in whole or in part, in any form or by any means, electronic or mechanical, including photocopying, recording, or by any information storage and retrieval system, without permission in writing from the Publisher.

Copyright © 2024 by
## National Learning Corporation

212 Michael Drive, Syosset, NY 11791
(516) 921-8888 • www.passbooks.com
E-mail: info@passbooks.com

PUBLISHED IN THE UNITED STATES OF AMERICA

# PASSBOOK® SERIES

THE *PASSBOOK® SERIES* has been created to prepare applicants and candidates for the ultimate academic battlefield – the examination room.

At some time in our lives, each and every one of us may be required to take an examination – for validation, matriculation, admission, qualification, registration, certification, or licensure.

Based on the assumption that every applicant or candidate has met the basic formal educational standards, has taken the required number of courses, and read the necessary texts, the *PASSBOOK® SERIES* furnishes the one special preparation which may assure passing with confidence, instead of failing with insecurity. Examination questions – together with answers – are furnished as the basic vehicle for study so that the mysteries of the examination and its compounding difficulties may be eliminated or diminished by a sure method.

This book is meant to help you pass your examination provided that you qualify and are serious in your objective.

The entire field is reviewed through the huge store of content information which is succinctly presented through a provocative and challenging approach – the question-and-answer method.

A climate of success is established by furnishing the correct answers at the end of each test.

You soon learn to recognize types of questions, forms of questions, and patterns of questioning. You may even begin to anticipate expected outcomes.

You perceive that many questions are repeated or adapted so that you can gain acute insights, which may enable you to score many sure points.

You learn how to confront new questions, or types of questions, and to attack them confidently and work out the correct answers.

You note objectives and emphases, and recognize pitfalls and dangers, so that you may make positive educational adjustments.

Moreover, you are kept fully informed in relation to new concepts, methods, practices, and directions in the field.

You discover that you are actually taking the examination all the time: you are preparing for the examination by "taking" an examination, not by reading extraneous and/or supererogatory textbooks.

In short, this PASSBOOK®, used directedly, should be an important factor in helping you to pass your test.

# SENIOR STATIONARY ENGINEER

## DUTIES

Senior Stationary Engineers under direction, are in responsible charge of the operation, maintenance and repair of all utilities in public buildings and of steam power plants, chiller plants, fire protection systems, swimming pools or indoor tennis courts. They take responsible charge of the operation, maintenance, testing and repair of plant equipment such as boilers, furnaces, refuse incinerators, pumps, fans, engines, turbines, generators, electrical equipment, heating and ventilating equipment, air conditioning and refrigeration systems; operate and/or supervise the operation of control consoles for building management and boiler management systems; troubleshoot problems with computerized controls, determine the source of the malfunction and take necessary steps to resolve the problem; are in responsible charge of operation, maintenance and repair of mechanical, electrical, and plumbing equipment in buildings; supervise assigned personnel; train staff in the operation, maintenance and use of equipment and systems; prepare work schedules and direct the assignment of personnel; work within budgetary guidelines; plan, allocate and maintain inventory and supplies for preventative and emergency maintenance needs; prepare equipment and material requisitions, including specifications and vendor bids required for operation, maintenance and repair; may prepare scope of work for vendor contracts; direct and evaluate studies of operating procedures for plant operation and maintenance; participate in the review of plans for new and/or rehabilitation construction projects and provide comments and recommendations; determine and direct work procedures and prioritize work in response to changing needs; ensure compliance with all jurisdictional codes; read plans and blueprints; keep records and write reports; may operate a motor vehicle in the performance of assigned duties. All Senior Stationary Engineers perform related work.

## THE TEST

The multiple-choice test may include questions on the operation, maintenance and repair of all utilities in large public buildings such as steam power and/or refuse incinerator plants, electrical systems and heating and ventilation equipment, supervision, personnel relations, job related calculations, and other related areas.

# HOW TO TAKE A TEST

I. YOU MUST PASS AN EXAMINATION

### A. WHAT EVERY CANDIDATE SHOULD KNOW

Examination applicants often ask us for help in preparing for the written test. What can I study in advance? What kinds of questions will be asked? How will the test be given? How will the papers be graded?

As an applicant for a civil service examination, you may be wondering about some of these things. Our purpose here is to suggest effective methods of advance study and to describe civil service examinations.

Your chances for success on this examination can be increased if you know how to prepare. Those "pre-examination jitters" can be reduced if you know what to expect. You can even experience an adventure in good citizenship if you know why civil service exams are given.

### B. WHY ARE CIVIL SERVICE EXAMINATIONS GIVEN?

Civil service examinations are important to you in two ways. As a citizen, you want public jobs filled by employees who know how to do their work. As a job seeker, you want a fair chance to compete for that job on an equal footing with other candidates. The best-known means of accomplishing this two-fold goal is the competitive examination.

Exams are widely publicized throughout the nation. They may be administered for jobs in federal, state, city, municipal, town or village governments or agencies.

Any citizen may apply, with some limitations, such as the age or residence of applicants. Your experience and education may be reviewed to see whether you meet the requirements for the particular examination. When these requirements exist, they are reasonable and applied consistently to all applicants. Thus, a competitive examination may cause you some uneasiness now, but it is your privilege and safeguard.

### C. HOW ARE CIVIL SERVICE EXAMS DEVELOPED?

Examinations are carefully written by trained technicians who are specialists in the field known as "psychological measurement," in consultation with recognized authorities in the field of work that the test will cover. These experts recommend the subject matter areas or skills to be tested; only those knowledges or skills important to your success on the job are included. The most reliable books and source materials available are used as references. Together, the experts and technicians judge the difficulty level of the questions.

Test technicians know how to phrase questions so that the problem is clearly stated. Their ethics do not permit "trick" or "catch" questions. Questions may have been tried out on sample groups, or subjected to statistical analysis, to determine their usefulness.

Written tests are often used in combination with performance tests, ratings of training and experience, and oral interviews. All of these measures combine to form the best-known means of finding the right person for the right job.

## II. HOW TO PASS THE WRITTEN TEST

### A. NATURE OF THE EXAMINATION

To prepare intelligently for civil service examinations, you should know how they differ from school examinations you have taken. In school you were assigned certain definite pages to read or subjects to cover. The examination questions were quite detailed and usually emphasized memory. Civil service exams, on the other hand, try to discover your present ability to perform the duties of a position, plus your potentiality to learn these duties. In other words, a civil service exam attempts to predict how successful you will be. Questions cover such a broad area that they cannot be as minute and detailed as school exam questions.

In the public service similar kinds of work, or positions, are grouped together in one "class." This process is known as *position-classification*. All the positions in a class are paid according to the salary range for that class. One class title covers all of these positions, and they are all tested by the same examination.

### B. FOUR BASIC STEPS

#### 1) Study the announcement

How, then, can you know what subjects to study? Our best answer is: "Learn as much as possible about the class of positions for which you've applied." The exam will test the knowledge, skills and abilities needed to do the work.

Your most valuable source of information about the position you want is the official exam announcement. This announcement lists the training and experience qualifications. Check these standards and apply only if you come reasonably close to meeting them.

The brief description of the position in the examination announcement offers some clues to the subjects which will be tested. Think about the job itself. Review the duties in your mind. Can you perform them, or are there some in which you are rusty? Fill in the blank spots in your preparation.

Many jurisdictions preview the written test in the exam announcement by including a section called "Knowledge and Abilities Required," "Scope of the Examination," or some similar heading. Here you will find out specifically what fields will be tested.

#### 2) Review your own background

Once you learn in general what the position is all about, and what you need to know to do the work, ask yourself which subjects you already know fairly well and which need improvement. You may wonder whether to concentrate on improving your strong areas or on building some background in your fields of weakness. When the announcement has specified "some knowledge" or "considerable knowledge," or has used adjectives like "beginning principles of..." or "advanced ... methods," you can get a clue as to the number and difficulty of questions to be asked in any given field. More questions, and hence broader coverage, would be included for those subjects which are more important in the work. Now weigh your strengths and weaknesses against the job requirements and prepare accordingly.

#### 3) Determine the level of the position

Another way to tell how intensively you should prepare is to understand the level of the job for which you are applying. Is it the entering level? In other words, is this the position in which beginners in a field of work are hired? Or is it an intermediate or advanced level? Sometimes this is indicated by such words as "Junior" or "Senior" in the class title. Other jurisdictions use Roman numerals to designate the level – Clerk I, Clerk II, for example. The word "Supervisor" sometimes appears in the title. If the level is not indicated by the title, check the description of duties. Will you be working under very close supervision, or will you have responsibility for independent decisions in this work?

### 4) Choose appropriate study materials

Now that you know the subjects to be examined and the relative amount of each subject to be covered, you can choose suitable study materials. For beginning level jobs, or even advanced ones, if you have a pronounced weakness in some aspect of your training, read a modern, standard textbook in that field. Be sure it is up to date and has general coverage. Such books are normally available at your library, and the librarian will be glad to help you locate one. For entry-level positions, questions of appropriate difficulty are chosen – neither highly advanced questions, nor those too simple. Such questions require careful thought but not advanced training.

If the position for which you are applying is technical or advanced, you will read more advanced, specialized material. If you are already familiar with the basic principles of your field, elementary textbooks would waste your time. Concentrate on advanced textbooks and technical periodicals. Think through the concepts and review difficult problems in your field.

These are all general sources. You can get more ideas on your own initiative, following these leads. For example, training manuals and publications of the government agency which employs workers in your field can be useful, particularly for technical and professional positions. A letter or visit to the government department involved may result in more specific study suggestions, and certainly will provide you with a more definite idea of the exact nature of the position you are seeking.


## III. KINDS OF TESTS

Tests are used for purposes other than measuring knowledge and ability to perform specified duties. For some positions, it is equally important to test ability to make adjustments to new situations or to profit from training. In others, basic mental abilities not dependent on information are essential. Questions which test these things may not appear as pertinent to the duties of the position as those which test for knowledge and information. Yet they are often highly important parts of a fair examination. For very general questions, it is almost impossible to help you direct your study efforts. What we can do is to point out some of the more common of these general abilities needed in public service positions and describe some typical questions.

1) General information

Broad, general information has been found useful for predicting job success in some kinds of work. This is tested in a variety of ways, from vocabulary lists to questions about current events. Basic background in some field of work, such as sociology or economics, may be sampled in a group of questions. Often these are principles which have become familiar to most persons through exposure rather than through formal training. It is difficult to advise you how to study for these questions; being alert to the world around you is our best suggestion.

2) Verbal ability

An example of an ability needed in many positions is verbal or language ability. Verbal ability is, in brief, the ability to use and understand words. Vocabulary and grammar tests are typical measures of this ability. Reading comprehension or paragraph interpretation questions are common in many kinds of civil service tests. You are given a paragraph of written material and asked to find its central meaning.

3) Numerical ability
Number skills can be tested by the familiar arithmetic problem, by checking paired lists of numbers to see which are alike and which are different, or by interpreting charts and graphs. In the latter test, a graph may be printed in the test booklet which you are asked to use as the basis for answering questions.

4) Observation
A popular test for law-enforcement positions is the observation test. A picture is shown to you for several minutes, then taken away. Questions about the picture test your ability to observe both details and larger elements.

5) Following directions
In many positions in the public service, the employee must be able to carry out written instructions dependably and accurately. You may be given a chart with several columns, each column listing a variety of information. The questions require you to carry out directions involving the information given in the chart.

6) Skills and aptitudes
Performance tests effectively measure some manual skills and aptitudes. When the skill is one in which you are trained, such as typing or shorthand, you can practice. These tests are often very much like those given in business school or high school courses. For many of the other skills and aptitudes, however, no short-time preparation can be made. Skills and abilities natural to you or that you have developed throughout your lifetime are being tested.

Many of the general questions just described provide all the data needed to answer the questions and ask you to use your reasoning ability to find the answers. Your best preparation for these tests, as well as for tests of facts and ideas, is to be at your physical and mental best. You, no doubt, have your own methods of getting into an exam-taking mood and keeping "in shape." The next section lists some ideas on this subject.


IV. KINDS OF QUESTIONS

Only rarely is the "essay" question, which you answer in narrative form, used in civil service tests. Civil service tests are usually of the short-answer type. Full instructions for answering these questions will be given to you at the examination. But in case this is your first experience with short-answer questions and separate answer sheets, here is what you need to know:

**1) Multiple-choice Questions**
Most popular of the short-answer questions is the "multiple choice" or "best answer" question. It can be used, for example, to test for factual knowledge, ability to solve problems or judgment in meeting situations found at work.
A multiple-choice question is normally one of three types—
- It can begin with an incomplete statement followed by several possible endings. You are to find the one ending which *best* completes the statement, although some of the others may not be entirely wrong.
- It can also be a complete statement in the form of a question which is answered by choosing one of the statements listed.

- It can be in the form of a problem – again you select the best answer.

Here is an example of a multiple-choice question with a discussion which should give you some clues as to the method for choosing the right answer:

When an employee has a complaint about his assignment, the action which will *best* help him overcome his difficulty is to
   A. discuss his difficulty with his coworkers
   B. take the problem to the head of the organization
   C. take the problem to the person who gave him the assignment
   D. say nothing to anyone about his complaint

In answering this question, you should study each of the choices to find which is best. Consider choice "A" – Certainly an employee may discuss his complaint with fellow employees, but no change or improvement can result, and the complaint remains unresolved. Choice "B" is a poor choice since the head of the organization probably does not know what assignment you have been given, and taking your problem to him is known as "going over the head" of the supervisor. The supervisor, or person who made the assignment, is the person who can clarify it or correct any injustice. Choice "C" is, therefore, correct. To say nothing, as in choice "D," is unwise. Supervisors have and interest in knowing the problems employees are facing, and the employee is seeking a solution to his problem.

## 2) True/False Questions

The "true/false" or "right/wrong" form of question is sometimes used. Here a complete statement is given. Your job is to decide whether the statement is right or wrong.

SAMPLE: A roaming cell-phone call to a nearby city costs less than a non-roaming call to a distant city.

This statement is wrong, or false, since roaming calls are more expensive.

This is not a complete list of all possible question forms, although most of the others are variations of these common types. You will always get complete directions for answering questions. Be sure you understand *how* to mark your answers – ask questions until you do.


V. RECORDING YOUR ANSWERS

Computer terminals are used more and more today for many different kinds of exams.
For an examination with very few applicants, you may be told to record your answers in the test booklet itself. Separate answer sheets are much more common. If this separate answer sheet is to be scored by machine – and this is often the case – it is highly important that you mark your answers correctly in order to get credit.
An electronic scoring machine is often used in civil service offices because of the speed with which papers can be scored. Machine-scored answer sheets must be marked with a pencil, which will be given to you. This pencil has a high graphite content which responds to the electronic scoring machine. As a matter of fact, stray dots may register as answers, so do not let your pencil rest on the answer sheet while you are pondering the correct answer. Also, if your pencil lead breaks or is otherwise defective, ask for another.

Since the answer sheet will be dropped in a slot in the scoring machine, be careful not to bend the corners or get the paper crumpled.

The answer sheet normally has five vertical columns of numbers, with 30 numbers to a column. These numbers correspond to the question numbers in your test booklet. After each number, going across the page are four or five pairs of dotted lines. These short dotted lines have small letters or numbers above them. The first two pairs may also have a "T" or "F" above the letters. This indicates that the first two pairs only are to be used if the questions are of the true-false type. If the questions are multiple choice, disregard the "T" and "F" and pay attention only to the small letters or numbers.

Answer your questions in the manner of the sample that follows:

32. The largest city in the United States is
    A. Washington, D.C.
    B. New York City
    C. Chicago
    D. Detroit
    E. San Francisco

1) Choose the answer you think is best. (New York City is the largest, so "B" is correct.)
2) Find the row of dotted lines numbered the same as the question you are answering. (Find row number 32)
3) Find the pair of dotted lines corresponding to the answer. (Find the pair of lines under the mark "B.")
4) Make a solid black mark between the dotted lines.


## VI. BEFORE THE TEST

Common sense will help you find procedures to follow to get ready for an examination. Too many of us, however, overlook these sensible measures. Indeed, nervousness and fatigue have been found to be the most serious reasons why applicants fail to do their best on civil service tests. Here is a list of reminders:

- Begin your preparation early – Don't wait until the last minute to go scurrying around for books and materials or to find out what the position is all about.
- Prepare continuously – An hour a night for a week is better than an all-night cram session. This has been definitely established. What is more, a night a week for a month will return better dividends than crowding your study into a shorter period of time.
- Locate the place of the exam – You have been sent a notice telling you when and where to report for the examination. If the location is in a different town or otherwise unfamiliar to you, it would be well to inquire the best route and learn something about the building.
- Relax the night before the test – Allow your mind to rest. Do not study at all that night. Plan some mild recreation or diversion; then go to bed early and get a good night's sleep.
- Get up early enough to make a leisurely trip to the place for the test – This way unforeseen events, traffic snarls, unfamiliar buildings, etc. will not upset you.
- Dress comfortably – A written test is not a fashion show. You will be known by number and not by name, so wear something comfortable.

- Leave excess paraphernalia at home – Shopping bags and odd bundles will get in your way. You need bring only the items mentioned in the official notice you received; usually everything you need is provided. Do not bring reference books to the exam. They will only confuse those last minutes and be taken away from you when in the test room.
- Arrive somewhat ahead of time – If because of transportation schedules you must get there very early, bring a newspaper or magazine to take your mind off yourself while waiting.
- Locate the examination room – When you have found the proper room, you will be directed to the seat or part of the room where you will sit. Sometimes you are given a sheet of instructions to read while you are waiting. Do not fill out any forms until you are told to do so; just read them and be prepared.
- Relax and prepare to listen to the instructions
- If you have any physical problem that may keep you from doing your best, be sure to tell the test administrator. If you are sick or in poor health, you really cannot do your best on the exam. You can come back and take the test some other time.

## VII. AT THE TEST

The day of the test is here and you have the test booklet in your hand. The temptation to get going is very strong. Caution! There is more to success than knowing the right answers. You must know how to identify your papers and understand variations in the type of short-answer question used in this particular examination. Follow these suggestions for maximum results from your efforts:

### 1) Cooperate with the monitor
The test administrator has a duty to create a situation in which you can be as much at ease as possible. He will give instructions, tell you when to begin, check to see that you are marking your answer sheet correctly, and so on. He is not there to guard you, although he will see that your competitors do not take unfair advantage. He wants to help you do your best.

### 2) Listen to all instructions
Don't jump the gun! Wait until you understand all directions. In most civil service tests you get more time than you need to answer the questions. So don't be in a hurry. Read each word of instructions until you clearly understand the meaning. Study the examples, listen to all announcements and follow directions. Ask questions if you do not understand what to do.

### 3) Identify your papers
Civil service exams are usually identified by number only. You will be assigned a number; you must not put your name on your test papers. Be sure to copy your number correctly. Since more than one exam may be given, copy your exact examination title.

### 4) Plan your time
Unless you are told that a test is a "speed" or "rate of work" test, speed itself is usually not important. Time enough to answer all the questions will be provided, but this does not mean that you have all day. An overall time limit has been set. Divide the total time (in minutes) by the number of questions to determine the approximate time you have for each question.

### 5) Do not linger over difficult questions

If you come across a difficult question, mark it with a paper clip (useful to have along) and come back to it when you have been through the booklet. One caution if you do this – be sure to skip a number on your answer sheet as well. Check often to be sure that you have not lost your place and that you are marking in the row numbered the same as the question you are answering.

### 6) Read the questions

Be sure you know what the question asks! Many capable people are unsuccessful because they failed to *read* the questions correctly.

### 7) Answer all questions

Unless you have been instructed that a penalty will be deducted for incorrect answers, it is better to guess than to omit a question.

### 8) Speed tests

It is often better NOT to guess on speed tests. It has been found that on timed tests people are tempted to spend the last few seconds before time is called in marking answers at random – without even reading them – in the hope of picking up a few extra points. To discourage this practice, the instructions may warn you that your score will be "corrected" for guessing. That is, a penalty will be applied. The incorrect answers will be deducted from the correct ones, or some other penalty formula will be used.

### 9) Review your answers

If you finish before time is called, go back to the questions you guessed or omitted to give them further thought. Review other answers if you have time.

### 10) Return your test materials

If you are ready to leave before others have finished or time is called, take ALL your materials to the monitor and leave quietly. Never take any test material with you. The monitor can discover whose papers are not complete, and taking a test booklet may be grounds for disqualification.

## VIII. EXAMINATION TECHNIQUES

1) Read the general instructions carefully. These are usually printed on the first page of the exam booklet. As a rule, these instructions refer to the timing of the examination; the fact that you should not start work until the signal and must stop work at a signal, etc. If there are any *special* instructions, such as a choice of questions to be answered, make sure that you note this instruction carefully.

2) When you are ready to start work on the examination, that is as soon as the signal has been given, read the instructions to each question booklet, underline any key words or phrases, such as *least, best, outline, describe* and the like. In this way you will tend to answer as requested rather than discover on reviewing your paper that you *listed without describing*, that you selected the *worst* choice rather than the *best* choice, etc.

3) If the examination is of the objective or multiple-choice type – that is, each question will also give a series of possible answers: A, B, C or D, and you are called upon to select the best answer and write the letter next to that answer on your answer paper – it is advisable to start answering each question in turn. There may be anywhere from 50 to 100 such questions in the three or four hours allotted and you can see how much time would be taken if you read through all the questions before beginning to answer any. Furthermore, if you come across a question or group of questions which you know would be difficult to answer, it would undoubtedly affect your handling of all the other questions.

4) If the examination is of the essay type and contains but a few questions, it is a moot point as to whether you should read all the questions before starting to answer any one. Of course, if you are given a choice – say five out of seven and the like – then it is essential to read all the questions so you can eliminate the two that are most difficult. If, however, you are asked to answer all the questions, there may be danger in trying to answer the easiest one first because you may find that you will spend too much time on it. The best technique is to answer the first question, then proceed to the second, etc.

5) Time your answers. Before the exam begins, write down the time it started, then add the time allowed for the examination and write down the time it must be completed, then divide the time available somewhat as follows:
   - If 3-1/2 hours are allowed, that would be 210 minutes. If you have 80 objective-type questions, that would be an average of 2-1/2 minutes per question. Allow yourself no more than 2 minutes per question, or a total of 160 minutes, which will permit about 50 minutes to review.
   - If for the time allotment of 210 minutes there are 7 essay questions to answer, that would average about 30 minutes a question. Give yourself only 25 minutes per question so that you have about 35 minutes to review.

6) The most important instruction is to *read each question* and make sure you know what is wanted. The second most important instruction is to *time yourself properly* so that you answer every question. The third most important instruction is to *answer every question*. Guess if you have to but include something for each question. Remember that you will receive no credit for a blank and will probably receive some credit if you write something in answer to an essay question. If you guess a letter – say "B" for a multiple-choice question – you may have guessed right. If you leave a blank as an answer to a multiple-choice question, the examiners may respect your feelings but it will not add a point to your score. Some exams may penalize you for wrong answers, so in such cases *only*, you may not want to guess unless you have some basis for your answer.

7) Suggestions
   a. Objective-type questions
      1. Examine the question booklet for proper sequence of pages and questions
      2. Read all instructions carefully
      3. Skip any question which seems too difficult; return to it after all other questions have been answered
      4. Apportion your time properly; do not spend too much time on any single question or group of questions

5. Note and underline key words – *all, most, fewest, least, best, worst, same, opposite*, etc.
6. Pay particular attention to negatives
7. Note unusual option, e.g., unduly long, short, complex, different or similar in content to the body of the question
8. Observe the use of "hedging" words – *probably, may, most likely*, etc.
9. Make sure that your answer is put next to the same number as the question
10. Do not second-guess unless you have good reason to believe the second answer is definitely more correct
11. Cross out original answer if you decide another answer is more accurate; do not erase until you are ready to hand your paper in
12. Answer all questions; guess unless instructed otherwise
13. Leave time for review

   b. Essay questions
   1. Read each question carefully
   2. Determine exactly what is wanted. Underline key words or phrases.
   3. Decide on outline or paragraph answer
   4. Include many different points and elements unless asked to develop any one or two points or elements
   5. Show impartiality by giving pros and cons unless directed to select one side only
   6. Make and write down any assumptions you find necessary to answer the questions
   7. Watch your English, grammar, punctuation and choice of words
   8. Time your answers; don't crowd material

8) Answering the essay question

Most essay questions can be answered by framing the specific response around several key words or ideas. Here are a few such key words or ideas:

M's: manpower, materials, methods, money, management
P's: purpose, program, policy, plan, procedure, practice, problems, pitfalls, personnel, public relations

   a. Six basic steps in handling problems:
   1. Preliminary plan and background development
   2. Collect information, data and facts
   3. Analyze and interpret information, data and facts
   4. Analyze and develop solutions as well as make recommendations
   5. Prepare report and sell recommendations
   6. Install recommendations and follow up effectiveness

   b. Pitfalls to avoid
   1. *Taking things for granted* – A statement of the situation does not necessarily imply that each of the elements is necessarily true; for example, a complaint may be invalid and biased so that all that can be taken for granted is that a complaint has been registered

2. *Considering only one side of a situation* – Wherever possible, indicate several alternatives and then point out the reasons you selected the best one
3. *Failing to indicate follow up* – Whenever your answer indicates action on your part, make certain that you will take proper follow-up action to see how successful your recommendations, procedures or actions turn out to be
4. *Taking too long in answering any single question* – Remember to time your answers properly

## IX. AFTER THE TEST

Scoring procedures differ in detail among civil service jurisdictions although the general principles are the same. Whether the papers are hand-scored or graded by machine we have described, they are nearly always graded by number. That is, the person who marks the paper knows only the number – never the name – of the applicant. Not until all the papers have been graded will they be matched with names. If other tests, such as training and experience or oral interview ratings have been given, scores will be combined. Different parts of the examination usually have different weights. For example, the written test might count 60 percent of the final grade, and a rating of training and experience 40 percent. In many jurisdictions, veterans will have a certain number of points added to their grades.

After the final grade has been determined, the names are placed in grade order and an eligible list is established. There are various methods for resolving ties between those who get the same final grade – probably the most common is to place first the name of the person whose application was received first. Job offers are made from the eligible list in the order the names appear on it. You will be notified of your grade and your rank as soon as all these computations have been made. This will be done as rapidly as possible.

People who are found to meet the requirements in the announcement are called "eligibles." Their names are put on a list of eligible candidates. An eligible's chances of getting a job depend on how high he stands on this list and how fast agencies are filling jobs from the list.

When a job is to be filled from a list of eligibles, the agency asks for the names of people on the list of eligibles for that job. When the civil service commission receives this request, it sends to the agency the names of the three people highest on this list. Or, if the job to be filled has specialized requirements, the office sends the agency the names of the top three persons who meet these requirements from the general list.

The appointing officer makes a choice from among the three people whose names were sent to him. If the selected person accepts the appointment, the names of the others are put back on the list to be considered for future openings.

That is the rule in hiring from all kinds of eligible lists, whether they are for typist, carpenter, chemist, or something else. For every vacancy, the appointing officer has his choice of any one of the top three eligibles on the list. This explains why the person whose name is on top of the list sometimes does not get an appointment when some of the persons lower on the list do. If the appointing officer chooses the second or third eligible, the No. 1 eligible does not get a job at once, but stays on the list until he is appointed or the list is terminated.

## X. HOW TO PASS THE INTERVIEW TEST

The examination for which you applied requires an oral interview test. You have already taken the written test and you are now being called for the interview test – the final part of the formal examination.

You may think that it is not possible to prepare for an interview test and that there are no procedures to follow during an interview. Our purpose is to point out some things you can do in advance that will help you and some good rules to follow and pitfalls to avoid while you are being interviewed.

*What is an interview supposed to test?*

The written examination is designed to test the technical knowledge and competence of the candidate; the oral is designed to evaluate intangible qualities, not readily measured otherwise, and to establish a list showing the relative fitness of each candidate – as measured against his competitors – for the position sought. Scoring is not on the basis of "right" and "wrong," but on a sliding scale of values ranging from "not passable" to "outstanding." As a matter of fact, it is possible to achieve a relatively low score without a single "incorrect" answer because of evident weakness in the qualities being measured.

Occasionally, an examination may consist entirely of an oral test – either an individual or a group oral. In such cases, information is sought concerning the technical knowledges and abilities of the candidate, since there has been no written examination for this purpose. More commonly, however, an oral test is used to supplement a written examination.

*Who conducts interviews?*

The composition of oral boards varies among different jurisdictions. In nearly all, a representative of the personnel department serves as chairman. One of the members of the board may be a representative of the department in which the candidate would work. In some cases, "outside experts" are used, and, frequently, a businessman or some other representative of the general public is asked to serve. Labor and management or other special groups may be represented. The aim is to secure the services of experts in the appropriate field.

However the board is composed, it is a good idea (and not at all improper or unethical) to ascertain in advance of the interview who the members are and what groups they represent. When you are introduced to them, you will have some idea of their backgrounds and interests, and at least you will not stutter and stammer over their names.

*What should be done before the interview?*

While knowledge about the board members is useful and takes some of the surprise element out of the interview, there is other preparation which is more substantive. It *is* possible to prepare for an oral interview – in several ways:

**1) Keep a copy of your application and review it carefully before the interview**

This may be the only document before the oral board, and the starting point of the interview. Know what education and experience you have listed there, and the sequence and dates of all of it. Sometimes the board will ask you to review the highlights of your experience for them; you should not have to hem and haw doing it.

**2) Study the class specification and the examination announcement**

Usually, the oral board has one or both of these to guide them. The qualities, characteristics or knowledges required by the position sought are stated in these documents. They offer valuable clues as to the nature of the oral interview. For example, if the job involves supervisory responsibilities, the announcement will usually indicate that knowledge of modern supervisory methods and the qualifications of the candidate as a supervisor will be tested. If so, you can expect such questions, frequently in the form of a hypothetical situation which you are expected to solve. NEVER go into an oral without knowledge of the duties and responsibilities of the job you seek.

### 3) Think through each qualification required

Try to visualize the kind of questions you would ask if you were a board member. How well could you answer them? Try especially to appraise your own knowledge and background in each area, *measured against the job sought*, and identify any areas in which you are weak. Be critical and realistic – do not flatter yourself.

### 4) Do some general reading in areas in which you feel you may be weak

For example, if the job involves supervision and your past experience has NOT, some general reading in supervisory methods and practices, particularly in the field of human relations, might be useful. Do NOT study agency procedures or detailed manuals. The oral board will be testing your understanding and capacity, not your memory.

### 5) Get a good night's sleep and watch your general health and mental attitude

You will want a clear head at the interview. Take care of a cold or any other minor ailment, and of course, no hangovers.

*What should be done on the day of the interview?*

Now comes the day of the interview itself. Give yourself plenty of time to get there. Plan to arrive somewhat ahead of the scheduled time, particularly if your appointment is in the fore part of the day. If a previous candidate fails to appear, the board might be ready for you a bit early. By early afternoon an oral board is almost invariably behind schedule if there are many candidates, and you may have to wait. Take along a book or magazine to read, or your application to review, but leave any extraneous material in the waiting room when you go in for your interview. In any event, relax and compose yourself.

The matter of dress is important. The board is forming impressions about you – from your experience, your manners, your attitude, and your appearance. Give your personal appearance careful attention. Dress your best, but not your flashiest. Choose conservative, appropriate clothing, and be sure it is immaculate. This is a business interview, and your appearance should indicate that you regard it as such. Besides, being well groomed and properly dressed will help boost your confidence.

Sooner or later, someone will call your name and escort you into the interview room. *This is it.* From here on you are on your own. It is too late for any more preparation. But remember, you asked for this opportunity to prove your fitness, and you are here because your request was granted.

*What happens when you go in?*

The usual sequence of events will be as follows: The clerk (who is often the board stenographer) will introduce you to the chairman of the oral board, who will introduce you to the other members of the board. Acknowledge the introductions before you sit down. Do not be surprised if you find a microphone facing you or a stenotypist sitting by. Oral interviews are usually recorded in the event of an appeal or other review.

Usually the chairman of the board will open the interview by reviewing the highlights of your education and work experience from your application – primarily for the benefit of the other members of the board, as well as to get the material into the record. Do not interrupt or comment unless there is an error or significant misinterpretation; if that is the case, do not hesitate. But do not quibble about insignificant matters. Also, he will usually ask you some question about your education, experience or your present job – partly to get you to start talking and to establish the interviewing "rapport." He may start the actual questioning, or turn it over to one of the other members. Frequently, each member undertakes the questioning on a particular area, one in which he is perhaps most competent, so you can expect each member to participate in the examination. Because time is limited, you may also expect some rather abrupt switches in the direction the questioning takes, so do not be upset by it. Normally, a board member will not pursue a single line of questioning unless he discovers a particular strength or weakness.

After each member has participated, the chairman will usually ask whether any member has any further questions, then will ask you if you have anything you wish to add. Unless you are expecting this question, it may floor you. Worse, it may start you off on an extended, extemporaneous speech. The board is not usually seeking more information. The question is principally to offer you a last opportunity to present further qualifications or to indicate that you have nothing to add. So, if you feel that a significant qualification or characteristic has been overlooked, it is proper to point it out in a sentence or so. Do not compliment the board on the thoroughness of their examination – they have been sketchy, and you know it. If you wish, merely say, "No thank you, I have nothing further to add." This is a point where you can "talk yourself out" of a good impression or fail to present an important bit of information. Remember, *you close the interview yourself.*

The chairman will then say, "That is all, Mr. _____, thank you." Do not be startled; the interview is over, and quicker than you think. Thank him, gather your belongings and take your leave. Save your sigh of relief for the other side of the door.

*How to put your best foot forward*

Throughout this entire process, you may feel that the board individually and collectively is trying to pierce your defenses, seek out your hidden weaknesses and embarrass and confuse you. Actually, this is not true. They are obliged to make an appraisal of your qualifications for the job you are seeking, and they want to see you in your best light. Remember, they must interview all candidates and a non-cooperative candidate may become a failure in spite of their best efforts to bring out his qualifications. Here are 15 suggestions that will help you:

**1) Be natural – Keep your attitude confident, not cocky**

If you are not confident that you can do the job, do not expect the board to be. Do not apologize for your weaknesses, try to bring out your strong points. The board is interested in a positive, not negative, presentation. Cockiness will antagonize any board member and make him wonder if you are covering up a weakness by a false show of strength.

**2) Get comfortable, but don't lounge or sprawl**

Sit erectly but not stiffly. A careless posture may lead the board to conclude that you are careless in other things, or at least that you are not impressed by the importance of the occasion. Either conclusion is natural, even if incorrect. Do not fuss with your clothing, a pencil or an ashtray. Your hands may occasionally be useful to emphasize a point; do not let them become a point of distraction.

**3) Do not wisecrack or make small talk**

This is a serious situation, and your attitude should show that you consider it as such. Further, the time of the board is limited – they do not want to waste it, and neither should you.

### 4) Do not exaggerate your experience or abilities
In the first place, from information in the application or other interviews and sources, the board may know more about you than you think. Secondly, you probably will not get away with it. An experienced board is rather adept at spotting such a situation, so do not take the chance.

### 5) If you know a board member, do not make a point of it, yet do not hide it
Certainly you are not fooling him, and probably not the other members of the board. Do not try to take advantage of your acquaintanceship – it will probably do you little good.

### 6) Do not dominate the interview
Let the board do that. They will give you the clues – do not assume that you have to do all the talking. Realize that the board has a number of questions to ask you, and do not try to take up all the interview time by showing off your extensive knowledge of the answer to the first one.

### 7) Be attentive
You only have 20 minutes or so, and you should keep your attention at its sharpest throughout. When a member is addressing a problem or question to you, give him your undivided attention. Address your reply principally to him, but do not exclude the other board members.

### 8) Do not interrupt
A board member may be stating a problem for you to analyze. He will ask you a question when the time comes. Let him state the problem, and wait for the question.

### 9) Make sure you understand the question
Do not try to answer until you are sure what the question is. If it is not clear, restate it in your own words or ask the board member to clarify it for you. However, do not haggle about minor elements.

### 10) Reply promptly but not hastily
A common entry on oral board rating sheets is "candidate responded readily," or "candidate hesitated in replies." Respond as promptly and quickly as you can, but do not jump to a hasty, ill-considered answer.

### 11) Do not be peremptory in your answers
A brief answer is proper – but do not fire your answer back. That is a losing game from your point of view. The board member can probably ask questions much faster than you can answer them.

### 12) Do not try to create the answer you think the board member wants
He is interested in what kind of mind you have and how it works – not in playing games. Furthermore, he can usually spot this practice and will actually grade you down on it.

### 13) Do not switch sides in your reply merely to agree with a board member
Frequently, a member will take a contrary position merely to draw you out and to see if you are willing and able to defend your point of view. Do not start a debate, yet do not surrender a good position. If a position is worth taking, it is worth defending.

### 14) Do not be afraid to admit an error in judgment if you are shown to be wrong

The board knows that you are forced to reply without any opportunity for careful consideration. Your answer may be demonstrably wrong. If so, admit it and get on with the interview.

### 15) Do not dwell at length on your present job

The opening question may relate to your present assignment. Answer the question but do not go into an extended discussion. You are being examined for a *new* job, not your present one. As a matter of fact, try to phrase ALL your answers in terms of the job for which you are being examined.

*Basis of Rating*

Probably you will forget most of these "do's" and "don'ts" when you walk into the oral interview room. Even remembering them all will not ensure you a passing grade. Perhaps you did not have the qualifications in the first place. But remembering them will help you to put your best foot forward, without treading on the toes of the board members.

Rumor and popular opinion to the contrary notwithstanding, an oral board wants you to make the best appearance possible. They know you are under pressure – but they also want to see how you respond to it as a guide to what your reaction would be under the pressures of the job you seek. They will be influenced by the degree of poise you display, the personal traits you show and the manner in which you respond.


ABOUT THIS BOOK

This book contains tests divided into Examination Sections. Go through each test, answering every question in the margin. We have also attached a sample answer sheet at the back of the book that can be removed and used. At the end of each test look at the answer key and check your answers. On the ones you got wrong, look at the right answer choice and learn. Do not fill in the answers first. Do not memorize the questions and answers, but understand the answer and principles involved. On your test, the questions will likely be different from the samples. Questions are changed and new ones added. If you understand these past questions you should have success with any changes that arise. Tests may consist of several types of questions. We have additional books on each subject should more study be advisable or necessary for you. Finally, the more you study, the better prepared you will be. This book is intended to be the last thing you study before you walk into the examination room. Prior study of relevant texts is also recommended. NLC publishes some of these in our Fundamental Series. Knowledge and good sense are important factors in passing your exam. Good luck also helps. So now study this Passbook, absorb the material contained within and take that knowledge into the examination. Then do your best to pass that exam.

# EXAMINATION SECTION

# EXAMINATION SECTION
## TEST 1

DIRECTIONS: Each question or incomplete statement is followed by several suggested answers or completions. Select the one that BEST answers the question or completes the statement. *PRINT THE LETTER OF THE CORRECT ANSWER IN THE SPACE AT THE RIGHT.*

1. The MAIN function of a *steam separator* in a steam power plant is to

    A. reduce steam pressure
    B. remove excess oil vapors from the steam
    C. increase steam quality
    D. reduce back-pressure on the steam-driven equipment

2. The MAIN purpose of a *dip tube* in a low-pressure hot water system is to

    A. prevent air from entering the main
    B. determine the level of water in the boiler
    C. reduce air pollution
    D. eliminate condensation when starting up

3. The rating of a unit ventilator is USUALLY determined by a(n)

    A. anemometer          B. hydrometer
    C. psychrometer        D. ammeter

4. Of the following devices, the one that is used to record the air-flow-steam-flow relationship of a boiler in a steam plant is a

    A. Orsat analyzer      B. manometer
    C. steam-flow meter    D. heat meter

5. Of the following types of gas fuels, the one which has the HIGHEST BTU content per cubic foot is _____ gas.

    A. manufactured        B. coke-oven
    C. liquid petroleum    D. natural

6. Of the following gasket materials, the one which is BEST to use when oil at 300° F is being carried in a pipe is

    A. fiber and paper        B. synthetic rubber
    C. asbestos composition   D. corrugated copper

7. A monolithic repair of a slightly damaged sectional magnesia insulation covering is BEST made by

    A. wiring in a *Dutchman* and filling the voids with magnesia cement
    B. covering the damaged area with asbestos laminations
    C. filling in the broken portion with glass-fiber insulating cement
    D. replacing the entire section

8. Of the following piping materials, the one that should NOT be used in a fuel-oil piping system is

   A. galvanized iron
   B. type K copper tubing
   C. brass pipe
   D. steel pipe

9. A valve is marked *300 WOG.*
   This valve could NOT be properly used in a pipe conveying _____ pounds gage maximum.

   A. oil at 300
   B. air at 100
   C. water at 150
   D. steam at 300

10. A steam gage connection for a large boiler is connected to the top of the water column and is then brought down to the operating level 24 feet below. The gage actually reads 605 psi.
    The ACTUAL gage pressure in the boiler is MOST NEARLY _____ psi.

    A. 590    B. 595    C. 610    D. 620

11. Of the following types of industrial oil burners, the one that is COMPLETELY adaptable to fully automatic operation or wide variations in firing rate is the _____ burner.

    A. mechanical-pressure type
    B. air-atomizing
    C. steam-atomizing
    D. horizontal rotary-cup

12. A full backward curve type centrifugal fan is being used in a coal-fired power plant for forced draft. Assume that after adjusting the speed of the fan, it is still too high, resulting in more pressure than is necessary to overcome the resistance of the fuel bed and boiler. To correct this situation, it would be BEST to replace the fan with one of a _____ diameter, running at _____ rpm and with a _____ wheel.

    A. *smaller;* greater; wider
    B. *larger;* less; wider
    C. *larger;* greater; smaller
    D. *smaller;* less; smaller

13. Short stroking in a steam-driven reciprocating pump results in both a(n) _____ in steam consumption and a(n) _____ in pumping capacity.

    A. *decrease;* decrease
    B. *increase;* increase
    C. *decrease;* increase
    D. *increase;* decrease

14. Caustic embrittlement is the weakening of boiler steel as the result of inner crystalline cracks.
    This condition is caused by BOTH long exposure to

    A. a combination of stress and highly acidic water
    B. stress in the presence of free oxygen and highly acidic water
    C. a combination of stress and water with a pH of 7
    D. a combination of stress and highly alkaline water

15. Of the following statements pertaining to feedwater injectors, the one which is MOST nearly correct is that the injectors

    A. are very efficient pumping units
    B. are practical only on small boilers
    C. are very reliable in operation on all types of boilers
    D. can handle 250 to 300 degree water

16. In reference to power plant pumps, the letters N.P.S.H. are an abbreviation for

    A. Non Positive Static Head
    B. Net Position Static Head
    C. Non Positive Standard Head
    D. Net Positive Suction Head

17. A pump's maintenance is based on a preventive maintenance schedule. This means that the schedule should GENERALLY be determined by the

    A. actual time lapse between maintenance checks
    B. actual number of pump-operating hours
    C. pump's actual operating performance
    D. operating performance of the equipment connected to the pump

18. Periodic inspection and testing of mechanical equipment by the staff at a plant is done MAINLY to

    A. help the men to better understand the operation of the equipment
    B. keep the men busy during slack times
    C. encourage the men to better understand each others' working capabilities
    D. discover minor equipment faults before they develop into major breakdowns

19. In planning a preventive maintenance program, the FIRST step to be taken is to

    A. repair all equipment that is not in service
    B. check all fuel oil burner tips
    C. make an inventory of all plant equipment
    D. check all electrical wiring to motors

20. An electric motor having class A insulation has been permitted to operate continuously at rated load even though the internal insulation temperature reads 10C above the allowable maximum internal temperature. Operating at this excessive temperature WOULD

    A. require frequent lubrication of the motor bearings
    B. reduce the life expectancy of the electric motor
    C. require an increase in voltage
    D. reduce the power factor to one-half of its normal value

21. The synchronous speed of a three-phase squirrel cage induction motor operating from a fixed frequency system can ONLY be changed by altering the

    A. rated locked-rotor torque
    B. rheostat position of the unloaded machine
    C. brush holder position
    D. number of poles in the stator

22. A thermal overload relay on an electric motor has been frequently tripping out. Of the following actions, the BEST one to take first to correct this problem would be to

    A. bypass the relay
    B. block the relay on a closed position
    C. clean the relay contacts
    D. arbitrarily readjust the relay setting

22.____

23. An air heater for a steam generator providing combustion air at temperatures ranging upward from 300F will often effect savings in fuel ranging from

    A. 1 to 3%     B. 5 to 10%     C. 12 to 15%     D. 17 to 20%

23.____

24. You have been asked to make an inspection of the superheater of a steam generator for external corrosion. You should be aware that if the direction of gas flow perpendicular to a tangent to the superheater tube is considered to be the 12 o'clock position, the GREATEST metal loss due to external corrosion usually occurs on the _____ o'clock and _____ o'clock sectors of the tube.

    A. 12; 6     B. 10; 2     C. 8; 3     D. 7; 5

24.____

25. In the steam generating plant to which you are assigned, the starting-up time and the shutting-down time for the boiler is determined by the time required to limit the thermal stresses in the drums and headers. The drums and headers have rolled tube joints. The temperature change in saturated temperature per hour for limit controlled heating and cooling rates for this boiler is established at _____ change.

    A. 50° F     B. 75° F     C. 100° F     D. 200° F

25.____

---

# KEY (CORRECT ANSWERS)

| | | | |
|---|---|---|---|
| 1. C | | 11. D | |
| 2. A | | 12. B | |
| 3. A | | 13. D | |
| 4. C | | 14. D | |
| 5. C | | 15. B | |
| 6. C | | 16. D | |
| 7. A | | 17. B | |
| 8. A | | 18. D | |
| 9. D | | 19. C | |
| 10. B | | 20. B | |

21. D
22. C
23. B
24. B
25. C

# TEST 2

DIRECTIONS: Each question or incomplete statement is followed by several suggested answers or completions. Select the one that BEST answers the question or completes the statement. *PRINT THE LETTER OF THE CORRECT ANSWER IN THE SPACE AT THE RIGHT.*

1. Assume that the optimum pH level of boiler feedwater for a boiler installation ranges between 8.0 and 9.5.
   The alkalizer used in the feedwater treatment to maintain this optimum pH level SHOULD introduce

   A. an average amount of iron and copper corrosion products into the steam cycle
   B. an increase of partial pressure of the carbon dioxide in the steam
   C. the least amount of iron and copper corrosion products into the boiler cycle
   D. a control of corrosion rates by forming a coating on the surfaces contacted by the steam

   1._____

2. The ppm of sodium sulfite that can be *safely* used for the chemical scavenging of oxygen in boiler feedwater is DEPENDENT upon the

   A. steam output of the boiler
   B. boiler operating pressure
   C. number of boiler steam drums
   D. construction of the boiler

   2._____

3. Of the following piping materials, the one which is NOT generally used for pneumatic temperature control systems is

   A. copper         B. plastic
   C. steel          D. galvanized iron

   3._____

4. In accordance with recommended maintenance practice, thermostats used in a pneumatic temperature control system SHOULD be checked

   A. weekly         B. bi-monthly
   C. monthly        D. once a year

   4._____

5. Of the following, the BEST method to use to determine the moisture level in a refrigeration system is to

   A. weigh the drier after it has been in the system for a period of time
   B. visually check the sight glass for particles of corrosion
   C. use a moisture indicator
   D. test a sample of lubricating oil with phosphorus pentoxide

   5._____

6. A full-flow drier is USUALLY recommended to be used in a hermetic refrigeration compressor system to keep the system dry and to

   A. prevent the products of decomposition from getting into the evaporator in the event of a motor burn-out
   B. condense cut liquid refrigerant during compressor off cycles and compressor start-up
   C. prevent the compressor unit from decreasing in capacity
   D. prevent the liquid from dumping into the compressor crankcase

   6._____

7. An economizer in a steam boiler is used to raise the temperature of the

   A. combustion air for firing fuel oil utilizing some of the heat in the exit flue gases
   B. combustion air for firing fuel oil utilizing some of the heat in the exhaust steam from the turbines of steam engines
   C. boiler feedwater by utilizing some of the heat in the exit flue gases
   D. boiler feedwater by utilizing some of the heat in the exhaust steam from the turbines or steam engines

8. A mixed-base grease is a grease that is prepared by mixing lubricating oil with

   A. one metallic soap
   B. two metallic soaps
   C. a synthetic lubricant
   D. heavy gear oil

9. Of the following lubricants, the one which is classified as a circulating oil is _____ oil.

   A. turbine
   B. gear
   C. machine
   D. steam-cylinder

10. You are supervising the installation of a steam-driven reciprocating pump. The pump's air chamber is missing and you have to replace it with one with several salvaged ones. The salvaged air chamber selected should have a volume equal to MOST NEARLY _____ the piston displacement of the pump.

    A. half of
    B. 1 1/2 times
    C. 2 times
    D. 2 1/2 times

11. Economical partial-load operation of steam turbines is obtained by minimizing throttling losses.
    This is accomplished by

    A. reducing the boiler pressure and temperature
    B. throttling the steam flow into the uncontrolled set of nozzles
    C. dividing the first-stage nozzles into several groups and providing a steam control valve for each group
    D. controlling the fuel flow to the steam generator

12. You are ordering two pump wearing rings for a centrifugal pump.
    These rings are GENERALLY identified as

    A. two wearing rings
    B. one drive wearing ring and one casing wearing ring
    C. one casing wearing ring and one impeller wearing ring
    D. one first-stage wearing ring and one drive wearing ring

13. A thermo-hydraulic feedwater regulator is used to regulate the flow of water to a drum-type boiler. The amount of water input to the boiler is controlled *in proportion to* the

    A. boiler load
    B. setting of the feed pump relief valve
    C. amount of water in the outer tube that flashes into steam
    D. water level in the drum

14. The standard capacity rating conditions for any refrigeration compressor is _____ psig for the suction and _____ psig for the discharge.

    A. 5° F, 19.6; 86° F, 154.5
    B. 5° F, 9.6; 96° F, 154.5
    C. 10° F, 9.6; 96° F, 144.5
    D. 10° F, 19.6; 96° F, 134.5

15. Of the following, the MAIN purpose of a subcooler in a refrigerant piping system for a two-stage system is to

    A. reduce the total power requirements and total heat rejection to the second stage
    B. reduce total power requirements and return oil to the compressor
    C. improve the flow of evaporator gas per ton and increase the temperature
    D. increase the heat rejection per ton and avoid system shutdown

16. In large refrigeration systems, the USUAL location for charging the refrigeration system is into the

    A. suction line
    B. liquid line between the receiver shut-off valve and the expansion valve
    C. line between the condenser and the compressor
    D. line between the high pressure cut-off switch and the expansion valve

17. The effect of a voltage variation to 90 percent of normal voltage, for a compound wound DC motor, on the FULL load current is

    A. an increase in the full load current of approximately 10%
    B. a decrease in the full load current of approximately 10%
    C. zero
    D. a decrease in the full load current 20%

18. The purpose of a current-limiting reactor is to place an upper limit on the available short-circuit current that can occur under fault conditions.
    The reactor accomplishes this by contributing _____ to the circuit.

    A. additional capacitance
    B. reduced inductive reactance
    C. reduced capacitance
    D. additional inductive reactance

19. Alternating current electric motors are usually guaranteed to operate satisfactorily and to deliver their full horsepower PROVIDED the electrical power delivered to the motor is at the rated

    A. voltage and at plus or minus 5 percent frequency variation
    B. frequency and at a voltage 15 percent above or below rating
    C. voltage and at plus or minus 10 percent frequency variation
    D. frequency and at a voltage 20 percent above or below rating

20. A three-phase AC motor is connected to a 230 volt, three-phase, alternating current line. With this motor running at full load, the line current is found to be 20 amperes, with a power factor of 0.75.
    Under these conditions, the power, in kilowatts, supplied to this motor will be MOST NEARLY

    A. 3.5    B. 6.0    C. 10.5    D. 18.0

21. In accordance with the air pollution control code, no person shall cause or permit the emission of air contaminants from a boiler with a capacity of 500 million BTU per hour or more, if the air contaminant emitted has a sulfur dioxide content of MORE than _____ parts per million by volume of undiluted emissions measured at _____ percent excess air.

    A. 300; 15    B. 200; 10    C. 200; 15    D. 300; 10

22. Of the following statements concerning the requirements of the air pollution control code, the one which is the MOST complete and correct is that the owner of equipment

    A. and apparatus shall maintain such equipment and apparatus in good operating order by regular inspection and cleaning and by promptly making repairs
    B. shall maintain the equipment in good operating condition by making inspections and repairs on a regular basis
    C. and apparatus shall maintain the equipment and apparatus in operating condition by regular inspection and cleaning
    D. shall maintain such equipment in good working order by regular inspection and cleaning and by making repairs on a scheduled basis

23. Assume that one of your assistants was near the Freon 11 refrigeration system when a liquid Freon line ruptured. Some of the liquid Freon 11 has gotten into your assistant's right eye.
    Of the following actions, the one which you should NOT take is to

    A. immediately call for an eye specialist (medical doctor)
    B. gently and quickly rub the Freon 11 out of the eye
    C. use a boric-acid solution to clean out the Freon 11 from his eye
    D. wash the eye by gently blowing the Freon 11 out of his eye with air

24. Assume that a fire breaks out in an electrical control panel board.
    Of the following types of portable fire extinguishers, the BEST one to use to put out this fire would be a _____ type.

    A. dry-chemical          B. soda-acid
    C. foam                  D. water-stream

25. Assume that you are checking the water level in a boiler which is on the line in a power plant. Upon opening the gage cocks, you determine that the water level was above the top gage cock.
    Of the following actions, the BEST one to take FIRST in this situation would be to

    A. shut off the fuel and air supply
    B. surface-blow the boiler
    C. close the steam-outlet valve from the boiler
    D. increase the speed of the feedwater pump

# KEY (CORRECT ANSWERS)

1. C
2. B
3. C
4. D
5. C

6. A
7. C
8. B
9. A
10. D

11. C
12. C
13. D
14. A
15. A

16. B
17. A
18. D
19. A
20. B

21. B
22. A
23. B
24. A
25. C

# EXAMINATION SECTION
# TEST 1

DIRECTIONS: Each question or incomplete statement is followed by several suggested answers or completions. Select the one that BEST answers the question or completes the statement. *PRINT THE LETTER OF THE CORRECT ANSWER IN THE SPACE AT THE RIGHT.*

1. The one of the following gases which will NOT be found in the flue gases produced by the complete combustion of fuel oil is

    A. oxygen
    B. hydrogen
    C. nitrogen
    D. carbon dioxide

2. The amount of $CO_2$ in a flue gas sample is USUALLY stated in

    A. parts per million
    B. pounds
    C. percent
    D. pounds per mol

3. A change in the efficiency of combustion in a boiler can USUALLY be determined by comparing the previously recorded readings with the current readings of the

    A. stack temperature and $CO_2$
    B. Ringelman chart and $CO_2$
    C. stack temperature and CO
    D. over-the-fire draft and CO

4. The tube-metal temperature is appreciably higher in a superheater tube than in a boiler tube when they are both subjected to the same temperatures because the superheater tube

    A. outside gas film conductivity is higher than that of the boiler tube
    B. outside gas film conductivity is lower than that of the boiler tube
    C. inside vapor film conductivity is lower than the water film conductivity in the boiler tube
    D. inside vapor film conductivity is higher than the water film conductivity in the boiler tube

5. In a balanced draft furnace, the

    A. draft changes from positive to negative in the furnace
    B. breeching contains a barometric damper
    C. draft reading is negative at the furnace inlet
    D. draft reading is positive at the furnace outlet

6. The heating of a #6 fuel oil in an oil burner to a temperature higher than necessary solely for proper atomization is

    A. *desirable* because it can increase the burner capacity by increasing the specific volume of the oil
    B. *desirable* because it can increase the flame stability when vaporization occurs intermittently in the supply line to the burner

C. *undesirable* because it can decrease the burner capacity by decreasing the specific volume of the oil
D. *undesirable* because it can decrease the burner capacity by increasing the specific volume of the oil

7. In a cylindrical boiler drum, the ratio of the force tending to burst a longitudinal seam to the force tending to burst a circumferential seam is MOST NEARLY

   A.  1:1            B.  2:1            C.  3:1            D.  4:1

8. The one of the following actions an operator should NOT take to stop or decrease carry-over caused by foaming in a boiler is to

   A. lower the water level in the drum
   B. blow down the boiler
   C. increase the rate of chemical feed to the boiler
   D. reduce the steam output

9. The PRIMARY reason for treating de-aerated feedwater with sodium sulphite is to

   A. remove dissolved oxygen        B. control scale
   C. prevent carry-over             D. increase alkalinity

10. In accordance with recommended practice, a sample of boiler water for pH analysis should be taken

    A. immediately after chemicals are added to the feedwater
    B. just before bottom blowdown
    C. when the steaming rate is high
    D. prior to putting the boiler on the line

11. Of the following oil burner types, the one in which the return oil passes through the atomizer body is the

    A. rotary cup
    B. steam atomizing
    C. mechanical pressure atomizing
    D. air atomizing

12. One advantage that the mechanical pressure atomizing oil burner has over the steam atomizing oil burner is that, with the mechanical pressure atomizing oil burner, the

    A. required oil temperature is lower
    B. required pump pressure is lower
    C. range of capacity available is wider
    D. fuel is more accurately and uniformly metered

13. Of the following, the LEAST likely cause of faulty atomization of fuel oil in a rotary cup burner is

    A. too low an oil temperature
    B. carbon formation on the rotary cup
    C. too low an oil pressure
    D. insufficient secondary air

3 (#1)

14. The device which senses the presence of the burner flame in a rotary cup oil burner is    14._____

    A. mercury tube           B. lead sulfide cell
    C. vaporstat              D. selenium rectifier

15. The component present, in GREATEST amount by weight, in #6 fuel oil is    15._____

    A. carbon     B. hydrogen     C. nitrogen     D. oxygen

16. The explosion hazard in an oil-fired boiler is usually GREATEST when    16._____

    A. lighting off
    B. securing the boiler
    C. firing at 75% of rated load
    D. firing at 100% of rated load

17. Of the following, the one which is the MOST complete and correct statement of the function of an F and T steam trap is that it removes    17._____

    A. only condensate from a steam line
    B. both condensate and non-condensable gases from a steam line
    C. only non-condensable gases from a steam line
    D. both sediment and rust particles from a steam line

18. Fire actuated fusible plugs on boilers should be renewed AT LEAST once every _____ months.    18._____

    A. 12     B. 18     C. 24     D. 30

19. A safety valve on a boiler must reach its full lift when the pressure is no GREATER than _____ above its set pressure.    19._____

    A. 3%     B. 5%     C. 7%     D. 8%

20. A device used to calibrate a steam pressure gauge is the _____ tester.    20._____

    A. spring-scale           B. dead-weight
    C. live-load              D. in-line

21. The one of the following statements that is NOT correct concerning feedwater injectors is that they are    21._____

    A. inefficient pumping units
    B. practical only on large boilers
    C. highly efficient thermally
    D. unreliable when subjected to varying loads and pressures

22. A steam pressure gauge is located 10 feet below the point where the connection is made to the top of a boiler water column. If the absolute pressure in the steam drum is 125 psi, the pressure at the gauge will be MOST NEARLY _____ psig.    22._____

    A. 102     B. 116     C. 119     D. 148

23. When comparing the operation and maintenance of a Stirling boiler with that of an equivalent horizontal straight tube boiler, the one of the following statements that is MOST complete and accurate is:    23._____

A. It is much harder to get to the tubes of a Stirling boiler for maintenance work than to a straight tube boiler with box headers
B. A Stirling boiler will steam at a lower rate than a straight tube boiler
C. Leaks occur more frequently in a Stirling boiler than in a straight tube boiler
D. The water and steam circulation rates are greater in a Stirling boiler than in a straight tube boiler

24. A supplier quotes a list price of $68.00 less discounts of 25 and 20 percent for a replacement part.
The actual cost of this item is MOST NEARLY

    A. $31    B. $34    C. $37    D. $41

25. The MAIN reason for maintaining an air dome in a pressurized house tank is to

    A. increase the tank pressure above the pump pressure
    B. avoid frequent start-and-stop pump operation
    C. force the water up to the top floor
    D. aerate the water

26. In a magnetic across-the-line starter for a 10 hp motor connected to a 4-wire, 3-phase circuit with grounded neutral, the MINIMUM required number of over-current devices is

    A. one, in the neutral conductor
    B. two, in any two conductors except the neutral
    C. three, in all conductors except the neutral
    D. four, in all four conductors

27. In order to select the correct heaters for the equipment described in Question 26 from the controller manufacturer's chart, the MOST important information needed is the

    A. power factor            B. line voltage
    C. full-load motor current D. motor horsepower

28. An electric motor, which is direct-connected to a centrifugal pump on an integral machined base, is to be replaced. In order to minimize the labor involved in replacing the motor, the specifications should include

    A. end bell size       B. serial number
    C. NEMA frame size     D. shaft size

29. A squirrel cage induction motor is rated at 5 hp when connected to a 220-volt, 3-phase, 60-cycle service.
If this motor is connected to a 208-volt, 3-phase, 60-cycle circuit, the horsepower rating would

    A. remain constant
    B. be increased by approximately 5%
    C. be decreased by approximately 10%
    D. be decreased by approximately 30%

30. A 20 hp, 230-volt DC motor operates at 75% efficiency. The full-load current, in amperes, is MOST NEARLY

    A. 45    B. 65    C. 85    D. 115

31. In a cooling tower, the water is cooled MAINLY by

    A. condensation  B. conduction
    C. convection  D. evaporation

32. An economizer is used with a steam boiler in order to raise the temperature of the

    A. boiler feedwater by utilizing some of the heat in the exit flue gases
    B. boiler feedwater by utilizing exhaust steam from the turbines or steam engines
    C. air used for combustion of the fuel utilizing some of the heat in the exit flue gases
    D. air used for combustion of the fuel utilizing exhaust steam from the turbines or steam engines

33. A centrifugal boiler feed pump requires 5 hp to drive it at a certain speed, total head and quantity of water delivered.
    If the speed and the quantity of water delivered are doubled and the total head quadrupled, the horsepower required will be APPROXIMATELY

    A. 10  B. 20  C. 30  D. 40

34. In a centrifugal pump installation, the available net positive suction head is NOT affected by the

    A. suction piping size and length
    B. level of the liquid supply
    C. temperature of the liquid being pumped
    D. cavitation in the pump

35. In operating a closed water circulating system, it is good practice to

    A. treat the water chemically for corrosion control
    B. drain and flush the system regularly to control corrosion
    C. leave the system undisturbed because it is sealed and needs no maintenance
    D. replace the pump shaft seals every three months

36. The function of an unloader on an electric motor-driven air compressor is to

    A. release the pressure in the cylinders in order to reduce the starting load
    B. reduce the speed of the motor when the maximum pressure is reached
    C. prevent excess pressure in the receiver
    D. drain the condensate from the cylinder head

37. The MOST highly toxic of the following refrigerants is

    A. sulphur dioxide  B. ammonia
    C. methyl chloride  D. freon 12

38. The MOST important objective of a safety training program should be to motivate the worker to

    A. avoid tripping hazards
    B. use hand tools properly
    C. write a clear concise accident report
    D. be constantly alert to safety hazards

39. An automatically controlled circulating water pump in a domestic hot water system is started by a device when it senses a

   A. drop in the water pressure in the circulating line
   B. drop in the water temperature in the return line
   C. rise in the water pressure in the circulating line
   D. rise in the temperature in the return line

40. In performing a hydrostatic test on an existing power boiler, the required test pressure must be controlled so that it is NOT exceeded by more than

   A. 2%    B. 4%    C. 6%    D. 8%

41. A preventive maintenance program in a boiler room should provide for routine periodic replacement of

   A. programmer electronic tubes
   B. badly leaking boiler tubes
   C. electric motors
   D. safety valve springs

42. The FIRST step to take in planning a preventive maintenance program is to

   A. replace all electric wiring
   B. make an equipment inventory
   C. replace all pump seals
   D. repair all equipment which is not in operation

43. The MOST important consideration in a fire prevention program is to

   A. train the staff to place flammables in fireproof containers
   B. know how to attack fires regardless of size
   C. see that halls, corridors, and exits are not blocked
   D. detect and eliminate every possible fire hazard

44. The type of portable fire extinguisher recommended as MOST effective for putting out oil fires is the _____ type.

   A. pump tank           B. cartridge actuated
   C. soda acid           D. foam

45. Inspecting and testing of mechanical equipment is done periodically MAINLY to

   A. help the men become more familiar with the equipment
   B. keep the men busy during slack periods
   C. encourage the men to take better care of the equipment
   D. discover minor equipment faults before they develop into major breakdowns

46. During the first stage of the high air pollution alert, plans must be made in public buildings to discontinue on-site incineration and to provide personnel and space to store the quantity of refuse that could accumulate during a period of _____ day(s).

   A. 1    B. 2    C. 5    D. 7

47. The four stages of the warning system designated by the high air pollution alert warning system are:   47.____

    A. initial, chronic, acute, penetrating
    B. forecast, alert, warning, emergency
    C. light, medium, heavy, extra heavy
    D. early, moderate, severe, toxic

48. Unless a sulphur exemption certificate is obtained, the amount of sulphur in residual fuel oil burned for heating purposes is restricted to NOT MORE than   48.____

    A. 0.2%   B. 0.3%   C. 0.55%   D. 0.7%

49. Refuse burning equipment in public buildings other than central municipal incinerators may NOT be operated except during the hours between   49.____

    A. 7 A.M. and 12 Noon       B. 7 A.M. and 5 P.M.
    C. 9 A.M. and 3 P.M.        D. 8 P.M. and 11 P.M.

50. The air contaminant detector required in a boiler installation must be adjusted to cause an audible and/or visible signal upon the emission of an air contaminant whose density, on the standard smoke chart, is GREATER than   50.____

    A. No. 1   B. No. 2   C. No. 3   D. No. 4

# KEY (CORRECT ANSWERS)

| | | | | |
|---|---|---|---|---|
| 1. B  | 11. C | 21. B | 31. D | 41. A |
| 2. C  | 12. D | 22. B | 32. A | 42. B |
| 3. A  | 13. D | 23. D | 33. D | 43. D |
| 4. C  | 14. B | 24. D | 34. D | 44. D |
| 5. A  | 15. A | 25. B | 35. A | 45. D |
| 6. D  | 16. A | 26. B | 36. A | 46. C |
| 7. B  | 17. B | 27. C | 37. A | 47. B |
| 8. C  | 18. A | 28. C | 38. D | 48. B |
| 9. A  | 19. A | 29. C | 39. B | 49. B |
| 10. B | 20. B | 30. C | 40. A | 50. A |

# TEST 2

DIRECTIONS: Each question or incomplete statement is followed by several suggested answers or completions. Select the one that BEST answers the question or completes the statement. *PRINT THE LETTER OF THE CORRECT ANSWER IN THE SPACE AT THE RIGHT.*

1. The one of the following grades of fuel oil that contains the GREATEST heating value in BTU per gallon is  1.____

    A. #2  B. #4  C. #5  D. #6

2. When we say that a fuel oil has a high viscosity, we mean MAINLY that the fuel oil will  2.____

    A. evaporate easily
    B. burn without smoke
    C. flow slowly through pipes
    D. have a low specific gravity

3. The type of fuel oil pump GENERALLY used with a rotary cup oil burner system is the  3.____

    A. propeller pump  B. internal pump
    C. centrifugal pump  D. piston

4. No. 6 fuel oil flowing to a mechanical atomizing burner should be preheated to APPROXIMATELY  4.____

    A. 185° F  B. 115° F  C. 100° F  D. 80° F

5. The flame of an industrial rotary cup oil burner should be adjusted so that the flame  5.____

    A. has a yellow color with blue spots
    B. strikes all sides of the combustion chamber
    C. has a light brown color
    D. does not strike the rear of the combustion chamber

6. The location of the oil burner *remote control switch* should GENERALLY be  6.____

    A. at the boiler room entrance
    B. on the boiler shell
    C. on the oil burner motor
    D. on a wall nearest the boiler

7. With forced draft, the approximate wind box pressure in a single-retort underfeed stoker is NORMALLY  7.____

    A. 2"  B. 5"  C. 7"  D. 9"

8. The pressure over the fire in a coal-fired steam boiler with a balanced-draft system and natural draft is MOST NEARLY  8.____

    A. +.60"  B. +.50"  C. -.02"  D. -.70"

9. Three tons of coal with an ash content of 10% will yield a weight of ash of MOST NEARLY _____ lbs.  9.____

    A. 400  B. 500  C. 600  D. 700

10. To clean and spread the coal over the grates of a coal-fired boiler, you would use a tool known as a(n)

    A. hoe    B. extractor    C. lance    D. slice bar

11. To burn the volatile matter in coal MORE efficiently, one should

    A. mix peat with the coal
    B. supply overfire draft
    C. mix it with a lower grade of coal
    D. add moisture to the coal

12. The one of the following that lists the size classifications of anthracite coal in proper order ranging from the smallest to the largest is:

    A. Chestnut, culm, pea, birdseye, egg
    B. Egg, stove, pea, broken, culm
    C. Stove, egg, birdseye, culm, broken
    D. Birdseye, pea, chestnut, stove, egg

13. The fire in a hand-fired furnace can be cleaned by a method known as

    A. ashpit to grate    B. bottom to top
    C. side to side    D. grate to crown

14. Coal is normally *tempered* when operating a chain-grate stoker for the purpose of

    A. increasing coking    B. preventing clinking
    C. collecting particles    D. promoting uniform burning

15. The one of the following coals that can legally be burned in power plants is

    A. anthracite    B. sub-bituminous
    C. non-coking    D. bituminous

16. The one of the following that is known as *rice coal* is _____ coal.

    A. pea    B. buckwheat #2    C. egg    D. culm

17. A MAJOR cause of air pollution resulting from the burning of fuel oils is _____ dioxide.

    A. sulphur    B. silicon    C. nitrous    D. hydrogen

18. The $CO_2$ percentage in the flue gas of a power plant is indicated by a

    A. Doppler meter    B. Ranarex indicator
    C. microtector    D. hygrometer

19. The MOST likely cause of black smoke exhausting from the chimney of an oil-fired boiler is

    A. high secondary air flow    B. low stack emission
    C. low oil temperature    D. high chimney draft

20. The diameter of the steam piston in a steam-driven duplex vacuum pump whose dimensions are given as 3 by 2 by 4 is

    A. 2    B. 3    C. 4    D. 6

21. An induced draft fan is GENERALLY connected between the

    A. condenser and the first pass
    B. stack and the breeching
    C. feedwater heater and the boiler feed pump
    D. combustion chamber and fuel oil tanks

22. The PURPOSE of an air chamber on a reciprocating water pump is to

    A. maintain a uniform flow
    B. reduce the amount of steam expansion
    C. create a pulsating flow
    D. vary the amount of steam admission

23. *Flash point* is the temperature at which oil will

    A. change completely to vapor
    B. safely fire in a furnace
    C. flash into flame if a lighted match is passed just above the top of the oil
    D. burn intermittently when ignited

24. A *sounding box* would NORMALLY be found

    A. on top of the boiler
    B. next to a compressed air tank
    C. in a fuel oil tank
    D. in a steam condenser

25. An *intercooler* is GENERALLY found on a(n)

    A. steam pump             B. air compressor
    C. steam engine           D. rotary oil pump

26. The instrument used to measure atmospheric pressure is a

    A. capillary tube         B. venturi
    C. barometer              D. calorimeter

27. The control which starts or stops the operation of the oil burner at a pre-determined steam pressure is the

    A. pressuretrol           B. air flow interlock
    C. transformer            D. magnetic oil valve

28. In a closed feedwater heater, the water and the steam

    A. come into direct contact
    B. are kept apart from each other
    C. are under negative pressure
    D. mix and exhaust to the atmosphere

29. A *knocking* noise in steam lines is GENERALLY the result of

    A. superheated steam expansion
    B. high steam pressure

C. condensation in the line
D. rapid steam expansion

30. An electrical component known as a step-up transformer operates by

    A. raising voltage and decreasing amperage
    B. decreasing amperage and raising resistance
    C. raising amperage and decreasing resistance
    D. raising voltage and amperage at the same time

31. A monometer is an instrument that is used to measure

    A. heat radiation                B. air volume
    C. eondensate water level        D. air pressure

32. Three 75-gallon per hour mechanical pressure type oil burners operating together are to burn 150,000 gallons of No. 6 fuel oil.
    The number of hours they would take to burn this amount of oil is MOST NEARLY

    A. 665        B. 760        C. 870        D. 1210

33. The sum of 10 1/2, 8 3/4, 5 1/2, and 2 1/4 is

    A. 23         B. 25         C. 26         D. 27

34. A water tank measures 50 feet long, 16 feet wide, and 12 feet high. Assume that water weighs 60 pounds per cubic foot and that one gallon of water weighs 8 pounds.
    The number of gallons the tank can hold when it is half full is

    A. 21,500     B. 28,375     C. 33,410     D. 36,000

35. Assuming 70 gallons of oil cost $42.00, then 110 gallons of oil at the same rate will cost

    A. $66.00     B. $84.00     C. $96.00     D. $152.00

Questions 36-40.

DIRECTIONS: Questions 36 through 40, inclusive, are to be answered in accordance with the information contained in the following paragraph.

*Fuel is conserved when a boiler is operating near its most efficient load. The efficiency of a boiler will change as the output varies. Large amounts of air must be used at low ratings and so the heat exchanger is inefficient. As the output increases, the efficiency decreases due to an increase in flue gas temperature. Every boiler has an output rate for which its efficiency is highest. For example, in a water-tube boiler, the highest efficiency might occur at 120 percent of rated capacity while in a vertical fire-tube boiler highest efficiency might be at 70% of rated capacity. The type of fuel burned and cleanliness affects the maximum efficiency of the boiler. When a power plant contains a battery of boilers, a sufficient number should be kept in operation so as to maintain the output of individual units near their points of maximum efficiency. One of the boilers in the battery can be used as a regulator to meet the change in demand for steam while the other boilers could still operate at their most efficient rating. Boiler performance is expressed as the number of pounds of steam generated per pound of fuel.*

36. According to the above paragraph, the number of pounds of steam generated per pound of fuel is a measure of boiler   36._____

    A. size
    B. performance
    C. regulator input
    D. by-pass

37. According to the above paragraph, the HIGHEST efficiency of a vertical fire-tube boiler might occur at   37._____

    A. 70% of rate capacity
    B. 80% of water tube capacity
    C. 95% of water tube capacity
    D. 120% of rated capacity

38. According to the above paragraph, the MAXIMUM efficiency of a boiler is affected by   38._____

    A. atmospheric temperature
    B. atmospheric pressure
    C. cleanliness
    D. fire brick material

39. According to the above paragraph, a heat exchanger uses large amounts of air at low   39._____

    A. fuel rates
    B. ratings
    C. temperatures
    D. pressures

40. According to the above paragraph, one boiler in a battery of boilers should be used as a   40._____

    A. demand    B. stand by    C. regulator    D. safety

# KEY (CORRECT ANSWERS)

| | | | |
|---|---|---|---|
| 1. D | 11. B | 21. B | 31. D |
| 2. C | 12. D | 22. A | 32. A |
| 3. B | 13. C | 23. C | 33. D |
| 4. A | 14. D | 24. C | 34. D |
| 5. D | 15. A | 25. B | 35. A |
| 6. A | 16. B | 26. C | 36. B |
| 7. A | 17. A | 27. A | 37. A |
| 8. C | 18. B | 28. B | 38. C |
| 9. C | 19. C | 29. C | 39. B |
| 10. A | 20. B | 30. A | 40. C |

# TEST 3

DIRECTIONS: Each question or incomplete statement is followed by several suggested answers or completions. Select the one that BEST answers the question or completes the statement. *PRINT THE LETTER OF THE CORRECT ANSWER IN THE SPACE AT THE RIGHT.*

1. The bottom blowdown on a boiler is used to

    A. remove mud drum water impurities
    B. increase boiler priming
    C. reduce steam pressure in the header
    D. increase the boiler water level

2. The term *spalling* refers to a boiler

    A. flue gas content
    B. soot blower
    C. combustion chamber
    D. mud leg

3. The wrench that would NORMALLY be used on hexagonally-shaped screwed valves and fittings is the _____ wrench.

    A. adjustable pipe
    B. tappet
    C. monkey
    D. open-end

4. The designated size of a boiler tube is GENERALLY based upon its

    A. internal diameter
    B. external diameter
    C. wall thickness
    D. weight per foot of length

5. A fusible plug on a boiler is made PRIMARILY of

    A. selenium      B. tin      C. zinc      D. iron

6. The range of *Ph* values for boiler feed water is NORMALLY

    A. 1 to 2      B. 4 to 6      C. 9 to 10      D. 12 to 15

7. The *boiler horsepower* is defined as the evaporation of _____ lbs. of water from and at 212° F.

    A. 900      B. 400      C. 345      D. 34.5

8. A low pressure air-atomizing oil burner has an operating air pressure range of _____ lbs.

    A. 25 to 35      B. 16 to 20      C. 6 to 10      D. 1 to 2

9. A superheater is installed in a Stirling boiler MAINLY for the purpose of raising the temperature of the

    A. secondary air
    B. steam leaving the steam drum
    C. boiler feed water
    D. primary air

23

10. The function of a counterflow economizer in a power plant is to

    A. use flue gases to heat feed water
    B. raise flue gas temperatures
    C. recirculate exhaust steam
    D. pre-heat combustion air

11. A fire due to spontaneous combustion would MOST easily occur in a pile of

    A. asbestos sheathing      B. loose lumber
    C. oil drums               D. oily waste rags

12. A *damper regulator,* used for combustion control, is operated by

    A. steam pressure          B. the water column
    C. the boiler pump         D. a pitot tube

13. The packing of an expansion joint in a firebrick wall of a combustion chamber is GENERALLY made of

    A. silica                  B. brick cement
    C. silicon carbide         D. asbestos

14. An open-ended steam pipe, called a steam lance, is USUALLY used on a boiler to

    A. remove soot             B. bleed the steam header
    C. clean the mud drum      D. clean chimneys

15. A high vacuum reading on the fuel oil gauge would indicate

    A. an empty oil tank       B. high oil temperature
    C. a clogged strainer      D. worn pump gears

16. The one of the following boilers that is classified as an internally-fired boiler is the _____ boiler.

    A. cross-drum straight tube
    B. vertical tubular
    C. Stirling
    D. cross-drum horizontal box-header

17. Try-cocks are used on a boiler PRIMARILY to

    A. check the gauge glass reading
    B. release steam pressure
    C. drain the water column
    D. blow down the gauge glass

18. Scale deposits on the tubes and shell of a high-pressure boiler are UNDESIRABLE because the deposits cause

    A. protrusions or roughness    B. suction
    C. foaming                     D. concentrates

19. The function of a radiation pyrometer is to measure

    A. boiler water height     B. boiler pressure
    C. furnace temperature     D. boiler drum stresses

20. An engine indicator is GENERALLY used to measure

    A. steam temperature
    B. heat losses
    C. errors in gauge readings
    D. steam cylinder pressures

21. A goose-neck is installed in the line connecting a steam gauge to a boiler to

    A. maintain constant steam flow
    B. prevent steam knocking
    C. maintain steam pressure
    D. protect the gauge element

22. A boiler steam gauge should have a range of AT LEAST

    A. one-half the working steam pressure
    B. the working steam pressure
    C. 1 1/2 times the maximum allowable working pressure
    D. twice the maximum allowable working pressure

23. A disconnected steam pressure gauge is USUALLY calibrated with a(n)

    A. Orsat instrument
    B. air pump
    C. tuyeres
    D. dead-weight tester

24. The recommended size joint for repairing firebrick wall is MOST NEARLY

    A. 1/64"     B. 1/16"     C. 1/4"     D. 1/2"

25. The acidity of boiler water is USUALLY determined by a _____ test.

    A. Rockwell
    B. soap hardness
    C. paper
    D. alkalinity

26. Electrostatic precipitators are used in power plants to

    A. remove fly ash from flue gases
    B. measure smoke conditions
    C. collect boiler impurities
    D. disperse minerals in feed water

27. Fly ash from the flue gases in a power plant is collected by a

    A. soot blower
    B. gas separator
    C. stack regulator
    D. mechanical separator

28. The installation of four new split packing rings in a stuffing box requires that the joints of the packing rings be placed _____ apart.

    A. 180°     B. 90°     C. 60°     D. 30°

29. In power plants, boiler feed water is chemically treated in order to

    A. prevent scale formation
    B. increase water foaming
    C. increase oxygen formation
    D. increase the temperature of the water

30. The soot in a fire tube boiler GENERALLY settles on the

    A. bridgewall
    B. inside tube surface
    C. combustion chamber sides
    D. outside tube surface

31. The one of the following classifications of fuel oil strainers that is generally NOT used with the heavier industrial fuel oils is a _____ strainer.

    A. wire mesh          B. metallic disc
    C. filter cloth       D. perforated metal cylinder

32. The temperature of the fuel oil leaving a pre-heater is controlled by a(n)

    A. potentiometer      B. relay
    C. low water cut-off  D. aquastat

33. A pneumatic tool is GENERALLY powered by

    A. natural gas    B. steam    C. a battery    D. air

34. The maximum steam pressure permitted in the steam coils used for heating the oil in a submerged oil storage tank is MOST NEARLY _____ psi.

    A. 40    B. 35    C. 25    D. 10

35. The water pressure used in a hydrostatic test on a boiler is GENERALLY _____ maximum working pressure.

    A. 4 times            B. 2 times the
    C. 1 1/2 times the    D. the same as

36. The one of the following valves that should be used in a steam line to throttle the flow is the _____ valve.

    A. plug    B. check    C. gate    D. globe

37. The CO (carbon monoxide) content in the flue gas from an efficiently fired boiler should be APPROXIMATELY

    A. 0% to 1%      B. 4% to 6%
    C. 8% to 10%     D. 12% to 13%

38. The $CO_2$ (carbon dioxide) percentage in the flue gas of an efficiently fired boiler should be APPROXIMATELY

    A. 1%    B. 12%    C. 18%    D. 25%

39. When the temperature of stack gases rises considerably above the normal operating stack temperature, it GENERALLY indicates

    A. a low boiler water level
    B. a heavy smoke condition in the stack
    C. that the boiler is operating efficiently
    D. that the boiler tubes are dirty

40. A boiler safety valve is USUALLY set above the maximum working pressure by an amount equal to _____ of the maximum working pressure.  40._____

    A. 6%  B. 10%  C. 12%  D. 14%

---

# KEY (CORRECT ANSWERS)

| | | | |
|---|---|---|---|
| 1. A | 11. D | 21. D | 31. C |
| 2. C | 12. A | 22. C | 32. D |
| 3. D | 13. D | 23. D | 33. D |
| 4. B | 14. A | 24. B | 34. D |
| 5. B | 15. C | 25. D | 35. C |
| 6. C | 16. B | 26. A | 36. D |
| 7. D | 17. A | 27. D | 37. A |
| 8. D | 18. A | 28. B | 38. B |
| 9. B | 19. C | 29. A | 39. D |
| 10. A | 20. D | 30. B | 40. A |

# EXAMINATION SECTION
# TEST 1

DIRECTIONS: Each question or incomplete statement is followed by several suggested answers or completions. Select the one that BEST answers the question or completes the statement. *PRINT THE LETTER OF THE CORRECT ANSWER IN THE SPACE AT THE RIGHT.*

1. Of the following, the one that is an *inherent* boiler heat loss is the loss due to

   A. dry chimney gases
   B. excess air
   C. unburned gaseous combustibles
   D. radiation from the furnace setting

   1.____

2. The one of the following flue gases whose presence indicates that MORE excess air is being supplied to a furnace than is being used is

   A. carbon dioxide          B. carbon monoxide
   C. nitrogen          D. oxygen

   2.____

3. A pressure gage on a compressed air tank reads 35.3 psi at 70° F.

   If, due to a fire, the temperature of the air in the tank were to increase to 600° F, the gage reading should be MOST NEARLY _____ psi.

   A. 70      B. 75      C. 80      D. 85

   3.____

4. Of the following types of flow meters, the one that is MOST accurate is a

   A. concentric orifice          B. venturi tube
   C. flow nozzle          D. pitot tube

   4.____

5. A spring pop safety valve on a fired high-pressure boiler fails to pop at its set pressure. Which of the following methods should be used to free the valve before retesting it?

   A. Strike the valve body with a soft lead hammer until it pops
   B. Raise the valve lifting-lever and release it
   C. Reduce the spring compression gradually until the valve opens
   D. Unscrew the valve one-quarter turn to relieve the strain on it

   5.____

6. A device which retains the desired parts of a steam-and-water mixture while rejecting the undesired parts of the mixture is a

   A. check valve          B. calorimeter
   C. stud tube          D. steam trap

   6.____

7. The MAIN advantage of using water-tube boilers in preference to fire-tube boilers in an installation is that water-tube boilers can be

   A. built much larger
   B. equipped with superheaters
   C. stoker-fired
   D. made portable

   7.____

8. The PRIMARY purpose of using phosphate to treat boiler water is to

   A. precipitate the hardness constituents
   B. scavenge the dissolved oxygen
   C. dissolve the calcium
   D. dissolve the magnesium

9. Assume that the set pressure of a safety valve on a power boiler is 100 psi. The MINIMUM pressure at which the safety valve must close after blowing down is _____ psi.

   A. 92      B. 94      C. 96      D. 98

10. A one-pound sample of wet steam at a certain pressure has an enthalpy of 960 BTU. For this same pressure, the Steam Tables list the enthalpy of saturated liquid as 130 and of saturated vapor as 1130 BTU.
    The quality of the sample steam is MOST NEARLY

    A. 75%     B. 85%     C. 90%     D. 95%

11. The type of feedwater heater which uses hot flue gases to heat the feedwater is known as a(n)

    A. economizer                B. direct-contact heater
    C. deaerator                 D. surface heater

12. The minimum recommended suction head for a centrifugal pump handling feedwater at 300° F is 155 feet.
    If the vapor pressure corresponding to the water temperature is 135 feet and the losses in the suction piping amount to 5 feet, the pump should be located AT LEAST _____ the lowest level of the water in the heater.

    A. 25 feet below             B. 15 feet below
    C. 15 feet above             D. 25 feet above

13. As compared to a power-driven triplex single-acting pump of the same size and operating at the same speed, a steam-driven duplex double-acting pump will

    A. pump more water per minute
    B. give a more uniform discharge
    C. have a higher first cost
    D. be more economical to operate

14. The MAIN advantage of operating a steam engine or steam turbine *condensing* is that it

    A. increases the mean effective pressure in the prime mover
    B. decreases the condensate temperature
    C. permits the use of exhaust steam to drive auxiliary equipment
    D. eliminates the need for separating non-condensibles from the steam

15. The automatic shut-off valves for a water gage installed on a high-pressure boiler must be _____ check valves.

    A. horizontal swing          B. vertical swing
    C. ball                      D. spring-loaded

16. The efficiency of a riveted joint is defined as the ratio of the

    A. plate thickness to the rivet diameter
    B. strength of the riveted joint to the strength of a welded joint
    C. strength of the riveted joint to the strength of the solid plate
    D. number of rivets in the first row of the joint to the total number of rivets on one side of the joint

17. A pump delivers 1500 pounds of water per minute against a total head of 200 feet. The water horsepower of this pump is MOST NEARLY

    A. 10  B. 40  C. 100  D. 600

18. In the most usual type of large capacity oil burner using #6 oil, under *fully automatic* control, the atomization of the oil is produced MAINLY by the

    A. pressure from the pump
    B. pressure from the secondary air fan
    C. oil temperature from the heater
    D. rotation of the burner assembly by the motor

19. Which of the following comes the closest to indicating the number of degree-days in a normal heating season in the city?

    A. 3000  B. 4000  C. 5000  D. 6000

20. In which of the following methods of steam generation would you expect to obtain reasonably continuous values of $CO_2$ CLOSEST to the perfect $CO_2$ value?
    Automatic

    A. stoker firing with temperature recorder
    B. stoker firing with *hold fire timer*
    C. oil firing with *stack switch*
    D. oil firing with *haze regulator*

21. The loss of heat in stack gases for heavy fuel oils is HIGHEST when the $CO_2$ content is _____ and the stack temperature is _____.

    A. 12%; 500°  B. 8%; 600°  C. 6%; 700°  D. 14%; 600°

22. A badly sooted HRT boiler under coal firing will show a _____ than a clean boiler.

    A. *higher* $CO_2$ value
    B. *lower* $CO_2$ value
    C. *higher* stack temperature
    D. *lower* draft loss

23. A unit heater condensing 50 lbs. of low pressure steam per hour would be rated MOST NEARLY at _____ square feet E.D.R.

    A. 50  B. 100  C. 150  D. 200

24. Which of the following values MOST NEARLY equals one horsepower?

    A. 550 ft.lbs. per sec.
    B. 3300 ft.lbs. per min.
    C. 5500 ft.lbs. per hour
    D. 10000 ft.lbs. per min.

25. An indicator card from a steam engine is most useful to the engineer in
   A. determining the boiler pressure
   B. determining the engine speed
   C. adjusting the valve setting
   D. computing the mechanical efficiency

## KEY (CORRECT ANSWERS)

1. A
2. D
3. D
4. B
5. B

6. D
7. A
8. A
9. C
10. B

11. A
12. A
13. A
14. A
15. C

16. C
17. A
18. D
19. C
20. D

21. C
22. C
23. D
24. A
25. C

# TEST 2

DIRECTIONS: Each question or incomplete statement is followed by several suggested answers or completions. Select the one that BEST answers the question or completes the statement. *PRINT THE LETTER OF THE CORRECT ANSWER IN THE SPACE AT THE RIGHT.*

1. A centrifugal water pump is direct-driven by a 25 HP 900 RPM electric motor at rated load.
   In order to double the quantity of water delivered, it would be necessary to substitute a motor rated at _____ HP at _____ RPM.

   A. 40; 1200   B. 50; 1200   C. 100; 1800   D. 200; 1800

2. The angle of advance of the eccentric on a D-slide valve steam engine is equal to

   A. the lead angle minus the lap angle
   B. the lead angle plus the lap angle
   C. 90 degrees minus the lead angle
   D. 90 degrees plus the lead and the lap angle

3. Of the following statements pertaining to a duplex steam-driven water pump, the one which is NOT true is that

   A. the slide valves have a steam and an exhaust lap
   B. there is a pause in the flow of water through the discharge valve at the end of the stroke
   C. the piston stroke can be adjusted
   D. an air chamber may be omitted on small sizes

4. The diagram on which a steam throttling process is indicated by a straight horizontal line is the _____ diagram.

   A. PV               B. Mollier
   C. Ringelman        D. temperature-entropy

5. The one of the following devices which is useful in preventing damage to a multi-stage turbine rotor due to unequal thermal expansion or contraction is the

   A. thrust bearing
   B. dummy piston and seal
   C. rupture seal
   D. motor-driven turning gear

6. The purpose of a steam turbine's governing system is to control steam flow through the unit, usually in order to keep some other factor constant.
   When a steam turbine is driving an alternator, the factor which is usually kept constant by the governor's operation is the

   A. inlet steam pressure      B. exhaust steam pressure
   C. shaft speed               D. power output

7. The speed regulation of a condensing steam turbine operating at 1800 RPM at no load and 1750 RPM at full load is MOST NEARLY

   A. 1%   B. 3%   C. 5%   D. 7%

8. The one of the following statements which is NOT true of the operation of steam turbines is that they

   A. operate most efficiently at high speed
   B. can be operated condensing or non-condensing
   C. can be used to drive centrifugal water pumps
   D. need high viscosity cylinder oil mixed with the steam supply to operate properly

9. Of the following, the one which is TRUE regarding backpressure steam turbines is that they

   A. operate on the exhaust steam from higher pressure turbines
   B. operate condensing
   C. exhaust through a very large hood
   D. convert a small part of the available heat in the steam into power

10. An aftercooler on a reciprocating air compressor is used PRIMARILY to

    A. increase compressor capacity
    B. improve compressor efficiency
    C. condense the moisture in the compressed air
    D. cool the lubricating oil

11. The one of the following tasks which is an example of preventive maintenance is

    A. replacing a leaking water pipe nipple
    B. cleaning the cup on a rotary cup burner
    C. cleaning a completely clogged oil strainer
    D. replacing a blown fuse

12. The four MAIN causes of failure of three-phase electric motors are

    A. dirt, friction, moisture, single-phasing
    B. friction, moisture, single-phasing, vibration
    C. dirt, moisture, single-phasing, vibration
    D. dirt, friction, moisture, vibration

13. Assume that an alternator running at a speed of 1800 RPM generates AC voltage at a frequency of 60 cycles per second (Hertz).
    The number of poles in this alternator is

    A. 2   B. 4   C. 6   D. 8

14. Assume that on an integrating watt-hour meter with 4 dials, the respective pointers from left to right are between 7 and 8, between 5 and 6, between 0 and 1, and between 3 and 4.
    Under these conditions, the reading is

    A. 8614   B. 7503   C. 3168   D. 3067

15. Assume that an ammeter is properly connected to a current transformer that has a ratio of 80 to 5. When the ammeter indicates 4.0 amperes, the current in the primary circuit is MOST NEARLY _____ amperes.

    A. 4.0   B. 20.0   C. 64.0   D. 80.0

16. Assume that two alternators, No. 1 and No. 2, are operating in parallel and that alternator No. 1 is taking a greater share of the load than alternator No. 2.
    Of the following, the PROPER method to reapportion the load between the two alternators is to

    A. speed up No. 2
    B. slow down No. 1
    C. increase the excitation of No. 2
    D. adjust the governors of both prime movers

17. Which of the following CORRECTLY describes the flow of electric power in a three-phase alternator?
    The input is _____ and the output is _____.

    A. three-phase AC to the stator; single-phase AC from the rotor
    B. three-phase AC to the rotor; single-phase AC from the stator
    C. DC to the stator; three-phase AC from the rotor
    D. DC to the rotor; three-phase AC from the stator

18. When the load on a mechanical stoker fired boiler plant furnishing steam for slide valve engine generators drops by 30%, the

    A. stoker should be shut down
    B. fan should be speeded up and the stoker slowed
    C. stoker should be speeded up and the air supply reduced
    D. stoker speed and air supply should be adjusted by reducing both

19. Which of the following statements is MOST NEARLY correct?

    A. All types of mechanical stokers may be used with equal efficiency under all types of boilers.
    B. Most stokers are designed with a weak member.
    C. The best type of stoker to use is not dependent upon the type of fuel available.
    D. The advisability of installing stokers is not dependent upon the load.

20. The number and size of safety valves required on a high pressure boiler is dependent upon the

    A. size of the boiler drums
    B. amount of heating surface
    C. number of pounds of fuel burned per square foot of grate per hour
    D. size of the steam main

21. In changing over a boiler from high pressure (150 lbs. per square inch) to 10 lbs. per square inch, it is USUALLY necessary to

    A. *increase* the size of the safety valves
    B. *decrease* the grate area
    C. *increase* the size of the feedwater piping
    D. *increase* the size of the blow down piping

22. A boiler feed injector becomes temporarily steam bound. To correct this condition, the MOST proper action to take is to

    A. increase boiler pressure
    B. reduce suction lift
    C. wrap it with cold rags
    D. bank fire

22.____

23. If in your plant the volume of air in cu.ft. per min. for combustion is represented by X, which of the following lowing values of X would MOST NEARLY represent the Cfm of stack gas, under usual conditions, that an induced draft fan would have to handle?

    A. X  B. 2X  C. 3X  D. 4X

23.____

24. If the stack switch of an oil burner becomes excessively sooted, a condition that is MOST likely to result is

    A. continuous shutting down of the burner shortly after it starts up
    B. excessive flow of oil to the burner resulting in a smoky fire
    C. excessive fire due to failure to cut off current to the burner motor
    D. failure of the warp switch of the relay to operate

24.____

25. In the usual high pressure electric generating plant in large buildings, heating the feedwater from 70° F to 180° F with exhaust steam usually will *decrease* the fuel consumption by

    A. 5%  B. 10%  C. 15%  D. 20%

25.____

## KEY (CORRECT ANSWERS)

| | | | |
|---|---|---|---|
| 1. D | | 11. B | |
| 2. B | | 12. D | |
| 3. A | | 13. B | |
| 4. B | | 14. B | |
| 5. D | | 15. C | |
| 6. C | | 16. D | |
| 7. B | | 17. D | |
| 8. D | | 18. D | |
| 9. D | | 19. B | |
| 10. C | | 20. B | |

21. A
22. C
23. B
24. A
25. B

# EXAMINATION SECTION
# TEST 1

DIRECTIONS: Each question or incomplete statement is followed by several suggested answers or completions. Select the one that BEST answers the question or completes the statement. *PRINT THE LETTER OF THE CORRECT ANSWER IN THE SPACE AT THE RIGHT.*

1. The capacity of a water-cooled condenser is LEAST affected by the        1.____

    A. surrounding air temperature
    B. water temperature
    C. refrigerant temperature
    D. quantity of water being circulated

2. The type of refrigeration system MOST commonly used in ice-skating rinks is the _____ system.        2.____

    A. direct expansion         B. simple secondary
    C. compound secondary       D. quadric resistance

3. The theoretical amount of refrigeration required to freeze one ton of water from 66° F to ice at 28° F in one day is _____ ton(s).        3.____

    A. 1.00       B. 1.25       C. 1.50       D. 1.75

4. The brine solution MOST commonly used in ice-skating rink piping, as a freezing medium, is a mixture of water and        4.____

    A. calcium chloride         B. sodium chloride
    C. glycol                   D. methanol

5. In an absorption refrigeration system, latent heat is absorbed by the refrigerant in the        5.____

    A. evaporator and the generator
    B. evaporator and the absorber
    C. condenser and the absorber
    D. condenser and the generator

6. Of the following refrigerants, the one which has the HIGHEST evaporator pressure at the standard 5° F temperature is        6.____

    A. ammonia                  B. freon 12
    C. methyl-chloride          D. carbon dioxide

7. The cooler in a refrigeration system that is equipped with automatic protective devices is MOST likely to be accidentally damaged by water freeze-up when the        7.____

    A. system is operating under reduced load
    B. system is operating at rated load
    C. system is being pumped down
    D. condenser cooling water flow is interrupted

2 (#1)

8. The one of the following statements pertaining to refrigerant compressor lubricants that is NOT true is that

    A. the type of oil that is used to lubricate centrifugal compressors can also be used in speed increasers
    B. ammonia causes very little viscosity change in lubricating oil
    C. most reciprocating compressors handling ammonia or freons can be lubricated properly with an oil having a viscosity of 300 Sec. SU @ 100° F
    D. freon 12 causes very little viscosity change in lubricating oil

8.____

9. The one of the following capacity controls which is USUALLY found in a refrigerant reciprocating-compressor system is a

    A. suction valve unloader
    B. throttling damper
    C. variable inlet guide vane
    D. condenser temperature control

9.____

10. A thermostatic expansion valve is connected to an evaporator operating at 5° F and 11.8 psig. The valve is in equilibrium at 10° superheat, and the pressure in the bulb is 17.7 psig.
    The EQUIVALENT valve-spring pressure on the refrigerant side of the sensitive element is _____ psi.

    A. 5.9     B. 10.9     C. 22.8     D. 29.5

10.____

11. A pressure gage on a compressed air tank reads 35.3 psi at 70° F.
    If, due to a fire, the temperature of the air in the tank were to increase to 600° F, the gage reading should be MOST NEARLY _____ psi.

    A. 70     B. 75     C. 80     D. 85

11.____

12. An ADVANTAGE that variable-speed control of a fan has over damper control is

    A. lower first-cost of controls
    B. lower power consumption
    C. cheaper fan drive motor
    D. constant high efficiency throughout entire fan load range

12.____

13. An intercooler is used on a two-stage air compressor to reduce the

    A. cylinder temperature in the first stage
    B. amount of condensate in the second stage
    C. back pressure of the air in the first stage
    D. work done on the air in the second stage

13.____

14. Of the following, the BEST instrument to use to measure small pressure differentials at low pressure is the

    A. mercury manometer           B. bourdon tube gage
    C. pressurtrol                 D. inclined manometer

14.____

15. A modulating pressurtrol on a boiler should contain a   15._____

    A. potentiometer  B. mercury switch
    C. manual reset lever  D. level indicator

16. Of the following automatic refrigerant expansion valves, the one which can only be used in a system where the liquid refrigerant can largely be stored in the evaporator without danger of sending slugs of liquid refrigerant over to the compressor is the _____ valve.   16._____

    A. thermal-expansion  B. diaphragm-expansion
    C. high-side float  D. low-side float

17. The refrigerating effect of a fluid is measured by the amount of heat it is capable of absorbing from the time it enters the   17._____

    A. evaporator as a liquid and leaves as a vapor
    B. condenser as a vapor and leaves as a liquid
    C. expansion valve as a liquid and leaves as a vapor
    D. compressor as a vapor and leaves as a vapor

18. The one of the following which lists the refrigerants in CORRECT order of decreasing toxicity is:   18._____

    A. Ammonia, sulphur dioxide, freon 12
    B. Sulphur dioxide, ammonia, freon 12
    C. Sulphur dioxide, freon 12, ammonia
    D. Ammonia, freon 12, sulphur dioxide

19. The one of the following methods which would MOST likely be used to control the capacity of a large centrifugal refrigerant compressor is the _____ method.   19._____

    A. cylinder unloader
    B. variable cylinder clearance
    C. variable speed
    D. stop and start

20. On a hot summer day, the GREATEST number of people working in a large air-conditioned office would feel comfortable if the temperature and relative humidity were maintained at   20._____

    A. 77° F and 50%  B. 80° F and 60%
    C. 74° F and 30%  D. 71° F and 50%

21. The one of the following conditions which has the GREATEST effect on the suction pressure on a swimming pool circulating pump is a   21._____

    A. clogged hair and lint strainer
    B. loss of coagulant
    C. low pH level
    D. clogged filter

22. A coagulant used in swimming pool filters is   22._____

    A. alum  B. chlorine
    C. soda-ash  D. sodium hypochlorite

23. According to the health code, the pH reading of swimming pool water should be between _____ and _____.   23.____

    A. 5.8; 6.4    B. 6.8; 7.4    C. 7.8; 8.4    D. 8.8; 9.4

24. An orthotolidine test is made to find out how much of which substance is contained in a sample of water?   24.____

    A. Alum    B. Ammonia    C. Chlorine    D. Soda-ash

25. The MINIMUM air temperature which must be maintained in an indoor swimming pool, except during the summer months, is _____ ° F.   25.____

    A. 68    B. 71    C. 75    D. 82

---

# KEY (CORRECT ANSWERS)

| | |
|---|---|
| 1. A | 11. D |
| 2. B | 12. B |
| 3. B | 13. D |
| 4. A | 14. D |
| 5. A | 15. A |
| 6. D | 16. C |
| 7. C | 17. A |
| 8. D | 18. B |
| 9. A | 19. C |
| 10. A | 20. A |

21. A
22. A
23. C
24. C
25. C

---

# TEST 2

DIRECTIONS: Each question or incomplete statement is followed by several suggested answers or completions. Select the one that BEST answers the question or completes the statement. *PRINT THE LETTER OF THE CORRECT ANSWER IN THE SPACE AT THE RIGHT.*

1. A permit is required for the storage or use of liquid chlorine.  1.____
   This permit is issued by which city agency?
   The

   A. Health Services Administration
   B. Board of Standards and Appeals
   C. Board of Water Supply
   D. Fire Department

2. The MINIMUM amount of free chlorine that swimming pool water should contain for  2.____
   proper disinfection is _____ part(s) per million.

   A. 1.0     B. 10     C. 40     D. 400

3. The agency which approves gas masks suitable for use in high concentrations of chlo-  3.____
   rine gas is the United States

   A. Environmental Protection Agency
   B. Department of Agriculture
   C. Bureau of Mines
   D. Department of Defense

4. The daily operational records of swimming pools which are required by the health code  4.____
   must be kept for a period of AT LEAST

   A. one month          B. six months
   C. one year           D. two years

5. The one of the following which is NOT used as a filtering media in swimming pool filters  5.____
   is

   A. sand               B. quartz
   C. diatomaceous earth D. clay

6. The point at which swimming pool filters should be back-washed is when the difference  6.____
   between the inlet and outlet pressure EXCEEDS _____ psi.

   A. 5     B. 10     C. 15     D. 20

7. Of the following valves, the type which can be used to adjust the rate-of-flow in a swim-  7.____
   ming pool filter is the _____ valve.

   A. butterfly          B. needle
   C. gate               D. stop-and-waste

8. When the coagulant in a swimming pool filter fails to jelly, the MOST likely cause of the  8.____
   failure is

   A. high water temperature           B. excess bacteria in the water
   C. insufficient alkalinity of the water  D. excess algae in the water

41

9. Of the following types of flow meters, the one that is MOST accurate is a

   A. concentric orifice
   B. venturi tube
   C. flow nozzle
   D. pitot tube

10. A spring pop safety valve on a fired high-pressure boiler fails to pop at its set pressure. Which of the following methods should be used to free the valve before retesting it?

    A. Strike the valve body with a soft lead hammer until it pops
    B. Raise the valve lifting-lever and release it
    C. Reduce the spring compression gradually until the valve opens
    D. Unscrew the valve one-quarter turn to relieve the strain on it

11. A device which retains the desired parts of a steam and water mixture while rejecting the undesired parts of the mixture is a

    A. check valve
    B. calorimeter
    C. stud tube
    D. steam trap

12. The PRIMARY purpose of using phosphate to treat boiler water is to

    A. precipitate the hardness constituents
    B. scavenge the dissolved oxygen
    C. dissolve the calcium
    D. dissolve the magnesium

13. The efficiency of a riveted joint is defined as the ratio of the

    A. plate thickness to the rivet diameter
    B. strength of the riveted joint to the strength of a welded joint
    C. strength of the riveted joint to the strength of the solid plate
    D. number of rivets in the first row of the joint to the total number of rivets on one side of the joint

14. A pump delivers 1500 pounds of water per minute against a total head of 200 feet. The water horsepower of this pump is MOST NEARLY

    A. 10    B. 40    C. 100    D. 600

15. A centrifugal water pump is direct-driven by a 25 HP 900 RPM electric motor at rated load.
    In order to double the quantity of water delivered, it would be necessary to substitute a motor rated at _____ HP at _____ RPM.

    A. 40; 1200    B. 50; 1200    C. 100; 1800    D. 200; 1800

16. Of the following fire extinguisher ratings, the one which indicates that an extinguisher has the GREATEST capability for extinguishing wood, paper, and electrical fires is

    A. 2-A:16-B:C
    B. 4-A:4-B:C
    C. 16-A
    D. 8-B

17. Of the following combinations of oil burners and fuel oils, the combination which is the MOST hazardous to fire-up when placing a cold boiler into service is the

    A. compressed air-atomized burner firing light oil
    B. steam-atomized burner firing heavy oil
    C. air-atomized burner firing heavy oil
    D. mechanically-atomized burner firing heavy oil

18. It is usually desirable to have a program which will create and maintain the interest of workers in safety. Of the following, the one which such a program CANNOT do is to

    A. develop safe work habits
    B. compensate for unsafe procedures
    C. provide a channel of communications between workers and management
    D. give employees a chance to participate in accident prevention activities

19. Because of a ruptured ammonia tank, the concentration of ammonia gas in a room exceeds 3%.
    The wearing of a gas mask, as the only protective device, by a person entering the room is

    A. *recommended,* because the gas mask alone is sufficient protection
    B. *not recommended,* because the ammonia will severely irritate the skin
    C. *not recommended,* because the gas mask is not effective at concentrations above 3%
    D. *not recommended,* because ammonia is flammable

20. The Occupational Safety and Health Act of 1970 provided for

    A. penalties against employees for safety violations
    B. complete occupational safety against all hazards
    C. standards of employee discipline
    D. employees' right to review a copy of a safety citation against the employer

21. An aftercooler on a reciprocating air compressor is used PRIMARILY to

    A. increase compressor capacity
    B. improve compressor efficiency
    C. condense the moisture in the compressed air
    D. cool the lubricating oil

22. The one of the following tasks which is an example of preventive maintenance is

    A. replacing a leaking water pipe nipple
    B. cleaning the cup on a rotary cup burner
    C. cleaning a completely clogged oil strainer
    D. replacing a blown fuse

23. The four MAIN causes of failure of three-phase electric motors are

    A. dirt, friction, moisture, single-phasing
    B. friction, moisture, single-phasing, vibration
    C. dirt, moisture, single-phasing, vibration
    D. dirt, friction, moisture, vibration

24. The one of the following electrical control components that may be lubricated is the

    A. drum controller's copper-to-copper contacts
    B. relay bearing
    C. starter silver contact
    D. shunt spring

25. In the planning of a preventive maintenance program, the FIRST requirement is to

    A. prepare a maintenance manual
    B. inventory the equipment
    C. inventory the tools available
    D. prepare repair requisitions for all equipment not operating satisfactorily

## KEY (CORRECT ANSWERS)

| | | | |
|---|---|---|---|
| 1. | D | 11. | D |
| 2. | A | 12. | A |
| 3. | C | 13. | C |
| 4. | B | 14. | A |
| 5. | D | 15. | D |
| 6. | B | 16. | B |
| 7. | A | 17. | D |
| 8. | C | 18. | B |
| 9. | B | 19. | B |
| 10. | B | 20. | D |

21. C
22. B
23. D
24. A
25. B

# EXAMINATION SECTION
## TEST 1

DIRECTIONS: Each question or incomplete statement is followed by several suggested answers or completions. Select the one that BEST answers the question or completes the statement. *PRINT THE LETTER OF TEE CORRECT ANSWER IN THE SPACE AT THE RIGHT.*

1. As a stationary engineer with an operating department, you are asked to consider the factors which should be taken into account in the selection of a new steam generator. Of the following, the one which has the LEAST effect upon the selection of a new steam generator (boiler) is the

    A. type of fuel to be used
    B. pressure and temperature of steam required
    C. expected steam load variations
    D. type of electrical energy to be generated, i.e., AC or DC

    1.____

2. Various authorities agree that *spalling* of the refractory lining in the furnace of a steam generator is said to exist when the *refractory cracks and breaks away at the surface*. A PRIMARY cause of spalling is

    A. uneven heating and cooling within the refractory brick
    B. continuous overfiring of the boiler
    C. slag accumulations on furnace walls
    D. change in fuel from solid to liquid type

    2.____

3. For laying-up a boiler for prolonged out of service periods, the alternate to the *dry method* is the *wet method*.
   The wet method provides that after the boiler has been completely cleaned and checked, it be filled to the vent valve with deaerated water to which a solution of caustic soda and sodium sulphite has been added.
   The pH value of this fluid in the boiler should be controlled and maintained in the range of

    A. 1 to 4      B. 3 to 6      C. 6 to 11      D. 13 to 14

    3.____

4. In a properly operated steam generator, the amount of blowdown is adjusted to some percentage of the steam flow, as approximated from tests, to keep the boiler-water solids concentration at or below some set limit.
   If we assume a limit of 850 ppm solids in boiler water, the 30% make up with 110 ppm solids, then for each 1000 lbs. of steam generated, the quantity of blowdown should be HOST NEARLY _____ ' lbs.

    A. 40      B. 60      C. 80      D. 100

    4.____

5. A steam generator is to be laid up for a rather long period of time. Of the several methods recommended for laying-up the boiler, the dry method is to be used, with the unit closed tightly.
   In this method, the drums and mud boxes are sealed after first placing trays of _____ in them.

    A. hot zeolite              B. unslaked lime
    C. trisodium phosphate      D. calcium chloride

    5.____

45

6. A given boiler is being fired in a proper manner for warm-up before being placed on the line. This boiler is one of a battery of four, all connected to the same header. This one boiler is equipped with a non-return valve.
   The purpose of this non-return valve is to prevent the flow of

   A. steam from the boiler until boiler pressure is above the header pressure
   B. feedwater from the boiler until boiler pressure is above the feedwater main pressure
   C. air into the boiler as it is being warmed up
   D. steam through the gauge glass in the event it should break

7. The PRIME fundamentals for proper and complete combustion are

   A. temperature and properly heated refractory
   B. time, temperature, and turbulence
   C. turbulence and forced draft
   D. turbulence, forced and induced draft, properly heated refractory, and non-slagging fly ash

8. In a given boiler, the lump size of bituminous coal is to be hand fired.
   Assuming that the grates have been properly designed and installed for firing this coal, the system of hand firing which should be used for MOST efficient combustion is the

   A. spreading method
   B. spreading method, along with occasional use of the alternate method
   C. alternate method, thereby doing away with the use of a slice bar
   D. coking method

9. The absorbing reagent which is used to absorb $CO_2$ is

   A. potassium pyrogallate
   B. cuprous chloride
   C. potassium hydroxide (caustic potash)
   D. hydrogen dioxide

10. The absorbing reagent which is used to absorb CO is

    A. hydrogen dioxide       B. potassium hydroxide
    C. potassium pyrogallate  D. cuprous chloride

11. The absorbing reagent which is used to absorb $O_2$ is

    A. potassium pyrogallate  B. potassium hydroxide
    C. cuprous chloride       D. hydrogen dioxide

12. Many factors are involved in the design of a furnace which should cover every possible operating condition.
    A device which is commonly used to preserve and prolong the life of furnace walls where furnace temperatures are high due to overfiring is the

    A. ignition-arch  B. bridgewall
    C. water-wall     D. back-arch

13. A poor grade of anthracite coal is properly burned in a furnace. A complete analysis of the flue gas is made.
    The one constituent which is probably present in this flue gas and which is potentially MOST corrosive is

    A. $H_2O$  B. CO  C. $SO_2$  D. $CO_2$

    13._____

14. Many existing steam generators which are coal fired (both hand and mechanical) are equipped with a system of balanced draft.
    With this system operating properly, the over fire draft should be MOST NEARLY _____ " w.g.

    A. +1.02  B. -1.02  C. -0.00  D. -0.02

    14._____

15. An operating boiler is generating superheated steam at 200 #/sq. and total temperature of 420° F. The operating engineer notes that the flue gas temperature in the stack is close to 1000° F. This unit is equipped with both an economizer and an air preheater. Of the following, the one set of conditions which is MOST likely NOT responsible for the 1000° F flue gas temperature is

    A. improper operation of the soot blower
    B. broken baffles in the boiler
    C. overfiring the boiler at a high rate in the flue gas
    D. a very high percentage of $CO_2$

    15._____

16. The manner in which fuel oils are treated before firing depends greatly on their viscosity. The MOST widely accepted standard test method which may be used to determine the viscosity of the various grades of fuel oil is commonly known as the _____ Universal Viscosimeter.

    A. Saybolt  B. Kinematic  C. Absolute  D. Potential

    16._____

17. A particular boiler is fired by means of straight mechanical pressure type (no return flow) burners using number 6 oil.
    The operating pressure range of these burners is such that atomization and operating characteristics become unstable if the pressure at the base of the nozzle falls below _____ psi.

    A. 180  B. 120  C. 50  D. 80

    17._____

18. A particular boiler has been designed for firing a small size of anthracite coal on a traveling grate stoker. This boiler furnace is provided with the new type rear arches.
    If we assume that moderately high grate speeds (approximately 40'/hr.) can be used, then the combustion rates can be anywhere from _____ lbs./sq.ft./hr.

    A. 5 to 10  B. 15 to 20  C. 30 to 40  D. 60 to 100

    18._____

19. With regard to the purchase of fuel oils, the *degree API at 60° F* is generally always given in the specification. With regard to this factor, one can always say that the calorific value in BTU gal will

    A. increase as the degree API at 60° F increases
    B. decrease as the degree API at 60° F increases

    19._____

C. not be affected by changes in the degree API at 60° F
D. increase as the degree API at 60° F rises to 25 and thereafter decrease

20. A recent development in the mechanical straight pressure type burner design is the use of a double tube gun. One tube is used to feed oil to the tip, and the other provides a passage for the unused oil to be returned.
In operation, with number 6 fuel oil, the important advantage of this design is that it

   A. gives good atomization with a wide variation in capacity
   B. permits the use of the flat flame as opposed to the hollow conical flame
   C. permits the use of a fuel oil piping system with both high and low suction lines
   D. allows the operator to fire fuel oil efficiently at reasonably low temperatures (approximately 120° F)

21. In order to fire fuel oil efficiently, it must be properly atomized immediately before it is mixed with the combustion air.
The type of fuel oil burner which is generally considered MOST costly to operate is a _____ atomizing burner.

   A. high-pressure air
   B. steam
   C. low-pressure air
   D. mechanical

22. Gasket materials, for use in making up pipe flanges, must be made of materials which will not be chemically or thermally affected by the fluid in the pipe.
Gaskets made of red rubber are MOST generally used for _____ for temperatures up to _____° F.

   A. oil; 200
   B. steam or water; 600
   C. water; 700
   D. air; 200

23. Gaskets made of corrugated copper are MOST generally used for _____ for temperatures up to _____° F.

   A. steam; 600
   B. steam or water; 1000
   C. oil; 1000
   D. steam, water, or oil; 1000

24. An industrial heating process in a given plant uses bled steam at 30 psi. Accurate and close temperature control is required for this process, and it is considered necessary that the steam trap used to drain condensate be of the continuously operating type.
Therefore, the type of steam trap which most definitely should NOT be used is the

   A. combination float and thermostatic
   B. thermostatic
   C. combination inverted bucket and thermostatic
   D. ball float with external thermostatic element

25. A deaerating type feedwater heater is now considered an essential piece of equipment in steam-electric generating stations. This is especially so if the generated steam pressures are comparatively high. This type of feedwater heater removes non-condensible gas such as air, free oxygen, carbon dioxide, etc.
If these are permitted to remain in the feedwater, they tend to

    A. gum up the feedwater strainers and pump valves
    B. increase scale formation and corrosion in the boilers
    C. increase *surging* in the boiler and *blistering* in the tubes
    D. destroy the lead metallic gaskets used in the pipe flanges

25._____

---

# KEY (CORRECT ANSWERS)

| | | | |
|---|---|---|---|
| 1. | D | 11. | B |
| 2. | C | 12. | C |
| 3. | D | 13. | C |
| 4. | A | 14. | D |
| 5. | B | 15. | D |
| 6. | A | 16. | A |
| 7. | B | 17. | C |
| 8. | D | 18. | D |
| 9. | C | 19. | A |
| 10. | D | 20. | A |

21. A
22. D
23. A
24. D
25. B

# TEST 2

DIRECTIONS: Each question or incomplete statement is followed by several suggested answers or completions. Select the one that BEST answers the question or completes the statement. *PRINT THE LETTER OF THE CORRECT ANSWER IN THE SPACE AT THE RIGHT.*

1. For a given plant, you are preparing to purchase valve seats and disks for the overhaul of the water end of a duplex direct-acting steam driven boiler feedwater pump. The material of which the valve disks should be made for this service is

   A. hard moulded rubber
   B. neoprene
   C. machined cast iron
   D. bronze

   1.____

2. Several types of duplex direct-acting steam driven pumps are in use for feedwater service in many steam generating plants. A basic difference relates to the use of the piston type and the outside packed plunger type pumps. From the point of view of the operating and maintenance personnel, in a given plant, the outside packed plunger type is considered more desirable.
   This opinion is acceptable because

   A. this type of pump is heavier and therefore more enduring
   B. for equal capacity, considerably less steam is used
   C. all packing leakage is external and is a guide for making adjustments
   D. plunger and packing friction is greatly reduced

   2.____

3. Pumps of the centrifugal type are generally manufactured in one of two general patterns, i.e., turbine with a diffuser ring, or volute without a diffuser ring. In the volute pattern pumps, the discharger chamber acts as a diffuser.
   The PRIMARY purpose of a diffuser ring or chamber is to

   A. convert high velocity to pressure
   B. convert high pressure to velocity
   C. convert the end thrust to a balanced side thrust
   D. bring about a balanced end thrust condition

   3.____

4. The recommended procedure for starting a turbine type centrifugal pump handling 100°F water which has a submerged suction is

   A. prime pump, start pump motor, open discharge valve, and then open suction valve
   B. open suction valve, start pump motor, when pump is up to speed gradually open the discharge valve
   C. open discharge valve, start pump motor, when pump is up to speed gradually open suction valve
   D. open discharge valve, start pump motor, prime pump, and then open suction valve gradually

   4.____

5. Some steam generating plants are equipped with injectors as standby equipment for their duplex direct-acting steam pumps. Assume that these injectors are of the single-tube lifting type.
   When one of these injectors is placed in operation, the steam will FIRST enter a(n)

   5.____

A. suction tube
B. combining tube
C. expanding nozzle
D. delivery tube

6. A duplex direct-acting steam driven pump with outside packed plungers is being put back in operation after being completely overhauled. As part of the overhaul work, the steam valves were replaced and set up with greatly reduced lost motion.
When this pump is started, the probability is that it will operate

A. at greatly reduced speed
B. at somewhat increased speed
C. with a short stroke
D. with a long stroke

6._____

7. Upon receiving a shipment of thermometers, you find that all of the instruments are calibrated with the centigrade instead of the fahrenheit scale.
If you had to use one of these thermometers to determine the temperature of boiler feedwater, then a reading of 55° centigrade would be equal to _____ ° fahrenheit.

A. 131　　B. 99　　C. 138.6　　D. 62.5

7._____

8. The water end of a duplex direct-acting steam driven plunger type boiler feedwater pump (double acting) has a bore of 3" and a stroke of 6". During the course of a one-hour test run, the speed is maintained constant at 50 rpm. Test data as follows is recorded:

　　Average water temperature　　　　　= 160° F
　　Total weight of water pumped　　　　= 16200#
　　Specific gravity 160° F　　　　　　　= 0.98
　　Weight of a gallon of water 160° F　　= 8.16#
　　Volume of one U.S. gallon　　　　　　= 231 cu.in.

Under the above conditions, the slip in this pump is MOST NEARLY _____ %.

A. 10　　B. 5　　C. 3　　D. 1/2

8._____

Questions 9-10.

DIRECTIONS: Questions 9 and 10 are to be answered on the basis of the following information.

The name plate data on a water tube boiler gives, in addition to the manufacturer's name, address, shop, and serial number, the following information:

　　Number of 4" tubes:　　- 60
　　Number of 2" tubes:　　- 150
　　Length of tubes:　　　 - 25'

Other data, such as total tube heating surface, boiler horsepower, etc. are so worn as to be unreadable. In operation, the boiler generates saturated steam at 125 psi. (The total heat required to generate a pound of steam under operating conditions is 1040 BTU/#.)

9. Disregarding drums, the total square footage of generating surface is MOST NEARLY

A. 41,000　　B. 18,100　　C. 9,100　　D. 3,500

9._____

10. Assume that the average heat transfer rate through the total tube surface is 3000 BTU sq.ft./hr. when operating at full load.
Under these conditions, the hourly steam generating rate becomes MOST NEARLY _____ #/hr.

    A. 26300   B. 10200   C. 52400   D. 118400

11. For a given ventilating system in a building, it is desired that the c.f.m. handled by the fan in the system be increased by 50%, i.e., from 8000 c.f.m. to 12000 c.f.m. The fan is motor driven by means of a v-belt drive. The present fan speed is 450 rpm.
In order to increase the fan output as given above, the new fan speed should be MOST NEARLY _____ rpm.

    A. 1010   B. 875   C. 750   D. 675

12. The following operating conditions exist for a given boiler:

    | | |
    |---|---|
    | Steam pressure | - 125#/sq.in. gauge |
    | Steam temperature (assume steam is delivered saturated and dry) | - 353° F |
    | Feedwater temperature | - 190° F |
    | Total heat of steam as delivered (enthalpy) | - 1193 BTU/# |
    | Heat of liquid at 190° F | - 158 BTU/# |
    | Calorific value of coal as fired | - 13000 BTU/# |

    As the result of the most recent test, the overall boiler efficiency is to be taken as 71%. In keeping with the above data, we may expect that for each pound of coal fired, the pounds of steam generated will be MOST NEARLY

    A. 10.91   B. 12.55   C. 8.91   D. 6.81

13. A given boiler, in operation, generates 50,000 # Hr. of steam at 200 #/sq.in. gauge, total temperature of 440° F, and total heat (enthalpy) of 1234.0. Feedwater is delivered to this boiler at a temperature of 190° F, and the heat of the liquid at this temperature is 158 BTU/#. The latent heat of vaporization for water at atmospheric pressure and 212° F is 970.3 BTU/#.
For the above outlined operating conditions, the Factor of Evaporation is MOST NEARLY

    A. 1.11   B. 1.27   C. 1.43   D. 0.903

14. After a good indicator card has been taken for a steam engine, the following equation is used to figure the Indicated Horsepower:

$$I.H.P = \frac{PLAN}{K}$$

    When N is given in rpm, then the numerical value of the constant K in the above equation is USUALLY equal to

    A. 5250   B. 33000   C. 1728   D. 550

15. A simplex double acting, horizontal, reciprocating steam engine is equipped with corliss type valve gear. This valve gear is of the releasing type.
In order to get a sharp out-off, _____ must be used.

A. a 600-w lubricant, to keep the valve gear free,
B. properly adjusted dashpots
C. a centrifugal inertia type governor
D. a single eccentric for control of all four valves

16. If a copper coil is rotated in a clockwise direction at a uniform speed in a uniform magnetic field, the induced voltage in the coil will be alternating in direction.
To obtain direct current from this coil when connected to an external circuit, it is common practice to use

   A. two slip rings
   B. one slip ring
   C. a commutator
   D. a balancer coil

17. Electrical apparatus such as a motor or generator which has been idle for some time in a damp location may have accumulated moisture and is, therefore, unsafe to put into operation. The apparatus should be dried out thoroughly before being returned to service and periodic insulation resistance measurements taken while in the process of drying out. This is done by using a(n)

   A. growler
   B. ammeter
   C. wattmeter
   D. megger

18. In reference to a dynamo, brush holders are used to guide and eliminate vibration of brushes, which is a common cause of sparking. The brushes are held against the commutator surface by adjustable springs.
For BEST operation, the spring tension should be adjusted so that brushes press against the commutator with a force of _____ lbs. per sq. in.

   A. 1.5 to 2.0
   B. 0.5 to 1.0
   C. 2.75 to 3.50
   D. 3.75 to 4.50

19. A power plant uses direct current generators to deliver electrical energy to a 3 wire balanced system of distribution.
Assuming that two (2) balance coils are used but are placed outside of the generator, then connection to the armature winding is USUALLY made through _____ slip ring(s).

   A. 2     B. 4     C. 1     D. 3

20. A steam engine is equipped with a flyball governor which is belt driven from a *driving* pulley mounted concentric with the engine shaft. This belt gives motion to a *receiving* pulley which is mounted on a stub shaft which, through bevel gears, gives motion to the governor shaft. Other things remaining the same, if the diameter of the receiving pulley is reduced, this engine would then MOST likely operate

   A. at a comparatively higher speed
   B. at the speed which existed before
   C. with a reduced cut-off
   D. at a comparatively lower speed

21. A nine stage impulse turbine is one in which the stationary vanes between the stages act to _____ the steam.

   A. reheat
   B. redirect
   C. re-expand
   D. recompress

22. A *rateau* or velocity stage is very often made part of a multi-stage impulse turbine. With respect to a nine stage impulse turbine, the velocity stage is GENERALLY the _____ stage.

    A. third  B. ninth  C. first  D. fifth

23. You are asked to assist in setting up and taking indicator cards for a corliss type steam engine. The steam line pressure is 200 psi, and the overall pencil rise of the indicator is 2 1/2".
    The BEST *scale of the indicator spring* which should be used, if the allowable pencil rise is limited to 2", is MOST NEARLY

    A. 40  B. 50  C. 100  D. 200

24. The design of a particular turbine is such that the critical speed is above the operating speed. Assume that you are assigned to place this turbine in operation. After warming up both the steam header and turbine, you slowly begin to bring the unit up to rated speed (3600 rpm). At approximately 1400 rpm, the turbine rotor begins to vibrate severely. As the operator, you should

    A. increase the speed rapidly and re-open the turbine drains
    B. check the overspeed trip to make sure no one has tampered with it
    C. check the lube oil pressure to make sure it is sufficiently high
    D. decrease the speed quickly and recheck drains, lube oil, and warm-up procedure

25. A steam engine having two cylinders side by side with the high-pressure cylinder exhausting into the low-pressure cylinder is an engine which is

    A. tandem-compound  B. cross-compound
    C. double           D. duplex

---

# KEY (CORRECT ANSWERS)

| | | | |
|---|---|---|---|
| 1. A | | 11. D | |
| 2. C | | 12. C | |
| 3. A | | 13. A | |
| 4. B | | 14. B | |
| 5. A | | 15. B | |
| 6. C | | 16. C | |
| 7. A | | 17. D | |
| 8. A | | 18. A | |
| 9. D | | 19. A | |
| 10. B | | 20. D | |

21. B
22. D
23. C
24. D
25. B

# TEST 3

DIRECTIONS: Each question or incomplete statement is followed by several suggested answers or completions. Select the one that BEST answers the question or completes the statement. *PRINT THE LETTER OF THE CORRECT ANSWER IN THE SPACE AT THE RIGHT.*

1. A steam generator is supplied with two safety valves on the boiler drum and one on the superheater section.
   The superheater safety valve would be relieved

   A. at the same pressure as those on the drum
   B. at a pressure higher than those on the drum
   C. at a pressure lower than those on the drum
   D. by a predetermined temperature element device

   1.____

2. The MAXIMUM size of blowdown piping for a boiler operating at 100 psi is _____ inch(es).

   A. 1    B. 1 1/2    C. 2 1/2    D. 4

   2.____

3. Superheater steam CANNOT be generated in a boiler due to

   A. inadequate heat in the fuel
   B. the presence of saturated water
   C. lifting of safety valves
   D. impurities in the water

   3.____

4. Which statement is MOST NEARLY correct?

   A. If a failure occurs in a water-tube boiler, it is less liable to explosion than a failure in a fire-tube boiler.
   B. It is safe to run a boiler at a higher pressure than that approved by the inspector.
   C. A dirty tube boiler produces steam as efficiently as a clean tube boiler.
   D. A boiler will operate efficiently with 1% CO.

   4.____

5. The Hartford loop is USUALLY used on a

   A. heating boiler        B. high pressure boiler
   C. refrigeration unit    D. compressor

   5.____

6. A fire-tube boiler, as compared to a water-tube boiler,

   A. is a faster steamer
   B. has a slower circulation rate
   C. is more economical
   D. can be made for high generation capacity rates

   6.____

7. On a B & W cross drum inclined water-tube boiler, sinuous or serpentine headers are used to

   A. provide greater strength in header with stays
   B. give better appearance
   C. allow for staggering the tubes in relation to each other
   D. allow for easier cleaning of soot from tubes

   7.____

8. Both ends of the straight tubes used in water-tube boilers are now customarily terminated in

   A. cylindrical drums with closed ends
   B. box headers
   C. sectional headers
   D. the steam drum

9. What would you use on an outside hand hole fitting on a sectional header of a cross drum water-tube boiler?
   A _____ gasket.

   A. raised lapped joint without a
   B. live thin rubber
   C. thin asbestos
   D. thin woven cotton

10. What is done BEFORE a hydrostatic test?

    A. Build a small fire in the boiler.
    B. Gag and clamp safety valves.
    C. Remove the water column.
    D. Increase the spring tension on safety valves.

11. On a 2" pop type safety valve set to blow at 280 psig, what is MOST NEARLY the total force, in lbs., on the seat of the valve at the time it starts to lift?

    A. 1100    B. 1000    C. 900    D. 600

12. The force required to lift a 3" safety valve with a pressure of 280 psi is _____ lbs.

    A. 840    B. 1979    C. 2520    D. 1680

13. A lever type safety valve has a 3" power arm, 4" diameter seat, and 24" weight arm. The weight necessary to allow the valve to lift at 50 psi is MOST NEARLY _____ lbs.

    A. 50    B. 60    C. 70    D. 80

14. In the sizing of anthracite coal, _____ is larger than _____ .

    A. nut; egg
    B. buckwheat no. 1; buckwheat no. 3
    C. stove; broken
    D. rice; pea

15. The size of anthracite coal which is between nut (chest-nut) and buckwheat #1 is known commercially as

    A. stove    B. pea    C. rice    D. barley

16. The MAXIMUM size opening in grate bars which should be used when burning pea coal is _____ inch.

    A. 3/4    B. 3/8    C. 5/8    D. 1/2

17. Buckwheat #3 coal is commercially known as 17.____

   A. rice  B. pea
   C. nonpareil  D. barley

18. On high pressure boilers, the water column is used in order to 18.____

   A. show directly to the operator the level of the water in the tubes
   B. find easily the pressure within the boiler
   C. dampen the oscillation of the water in the gauge glass
   D. prevent the boiler from exploding

19. Every power boiler must be provided with a steam gauge connected to the boiler steam 19.____
    space or to an intervening water column.
    The following equipment must be installed IMMEDIATELY before the gauge:

   A. Cock having a *T* or lever handle which is parallel to the connecting pipe when the cock is open
   B. Syphon to prevent the entrance of steam to the gauge
   C. 1/4 inch valved connection for attaching a test gauge when the boiler is operating
   D. all of the above

20. Why is a loop used on a steam gauge having a Bourdon tube? 20.____
    To

   A. allow for expansion and contraction
   B. stop fluctuation of steam pressure
   C. prevent hot steam from damaging the Bourdon tube
   D. prevent a slug of water from injuring the tube

21. Of the chemicals used in boiler water treatment, the one associated with oxygen removal 21.____
    is

   A. trisodium phosphate  B. potassium chromate
   C. sodium sulphite  D. magnesium sulphate

22. Organic compounds such as *tannins* and *quebracho* are often used in boiler water com- 22.____
    pounds containing soda ash or sodium phosphates.
    The purpose of the organic compounds is to

   A. reduce hydrolysis of softening chemicals
   B. disperse sludge formed by softening chemicals so they do not stick to heating surfaces
   C. soften water and remove oxygen
   D. form sludges and increase alkalinity

23. The chemical often used in boiler water treatment to coagulate and settle out solids in 23.____
    the boiler water, so that they may be removed by blowdown, is

   A. sodium aluminate  B. aluminum sulphate
   C. iron phosphate  D. sodium silicate

24. The Schneider method of determining the alkalinity concentration in boiler water consists of

    A. mechanical reproduction of the boiler water condition
    B. an electric method of measuring the conductivity
    C. a direct reading chemical determination by titration and neutralization
    D. utilization of improved methods of adding pyrites

25. Excessive amounts of boiler compound will lead to

    A. corrosion                     B. pitting
    C. caustic embrittlement    D. lower steam temperature

---

# KEY (CORRECT ANSWERS)

| | | | |
|---|---|---|---|
| 1. | C | 11. | C |
| 2. | C | 12. | B |
| 3. | B | 13. | D |
| 4. | A | 14. | B |
| 5. | A | 15. | B |
| 6. | B | 16. | D |
| 7. | C | 17. | D |
| 8. | C | 18. | A |
| 9. | D | 19. | D |
| 10. | B | 20. | C |

    21. C
    22. B
    23. A
    24. C
    25. C

# EXAMINATION SECTION
## TEST 1

DIRECTIONS: Each question or incomplete statement is followed by several suggested answers or completions. Select the one that BEST answers the question or completes the Statement. *PRINT THE LETTER OF THE CORRECT ANSWER IN THE SPACE AT THE RIGHT.*

1. The bottom blowdown on a boiler is used to

    A. remove mud drum water impurities
    B. increase boiler priming
    C. reduce steam pressure in the header
    D. increase the boiler water level

    1._____

2. The term *spalling* refers to a boiler

    A. flue gas content             B. soot blower
    C. combustion chamber           D. mud leg

    2._____

3. The wrench that would normally be used on hexagonally-shaped screwed valves and fittings is the _____ wrench.

    A. adjustable pipe              B. tappet
    C. monkey                       D. open-end

    3._____

4. The designated size of a boiler tube is GENERALLY based upon its

    A. internal diameter
    B. external diameter
    C. wall thickness
    D. weight per foot of length

    4._____

5. A fusible plug on a boiler is made PRIMARILY of

    A. selenium     B. tin     C. zinc     D. iron

    5._____

6. The range of pH values for boiler feed water is NORMALLY

    A. 1 to 2     B. 4 to 6     C. 9 to 10     D. 12 to 15

    6._____

7. The *boiler horsepower* is defined as the evaporation of _____ lbs. of water from and at 212° F.

    A. 900     B. 400     C. 345     D. 34.5

    7._____

8. A low pressure air-atomizing oil burner has an operating air pressure range of _____ lbs.

    A. 25 to 35     B. 16 to 20     C. 6 to 10     D. 1 to 2

    8._____

9. A superheater is installed in a Stirling boiler MAINLY for the purpose of raising the temperature of the

    A. secondary air                B. steam leaving the steam drum
    C. boiler feed water            D. primary air

    9._____

59

10. The function of a counterflow economizer in a power plant is to

    A. use flue gases to heat feedwater
    B. raise flue gas temperatures
    C. recirculate exhaust steam
    D. pre-heat combustion air

11. A fire due to spontaneous combustion would MOST easily occur in a pile of

    A. asbestos sheathing           B. loose lumber
    C. oil drums                    D. oily waste rags

12. A *damper regulator,* used for combustion control, is operated by

    A. steam pressure               B. the water column
    C. the boiler pump              D. a pitot tube

13. The packing of an expansion joint in a firebrick wall of a combustion chamber is GENERALLY made of

    A. silica                       B. brick cement
    C. silicon carbide              D. asbestos

14. An open-ended steam pipe, called a steam lance, is USUALLY used on a boiler to

    A. remove soot                  B. bleed the steam header
    C. clean the mud drum           D. clean chimneys

15. A high vacuum reading on the fuel oil gauge would indicate

    A. an empty oil tank            B. high oil temperature
    C. a clogged strainer           D. worn pump gears

16. The one of the following boilers that is classified as an internally fired boiler is the _____ boiler.

    A. cross-drum straight tube
    B. vertical tubular
    C. Stirling
    D. cross-drum horizontal box-header

17. Try-cocks are used on a boiler PRIMARILY to

    A. check the gauge glass reading
    B. release steam pressure
    C. drain the water column
    D. blow down the gauge glass

18. Scale deposits on the tubes and shell of a high-pressure boiler are UNDESIRABLE because the deposits cause

    A. protrusions or roughness     B. suction
    C. foaming                      D. concentrates

19. The function of a radiation pyrometer is to measure

   A. boiler water height
   B. boiler pressure
   C. furnace temperature
   D. boiler drum stresses

20. An engine indicator is GENERALLY used to measure

   A. steam temperature
   B. heat losses
   C. errors in gauge readings
   D. steam cylinder pressures

21. A goose-neck is installed in the line connecting a steam gauge to a boiler to

   A. maintain constant steam flow
   B. prevent steam knocking
   C. maintain steam pressure
   D. protect the gauge element

22. A boiler steam gauge should have a range of AT LEAST

   A. one-half the working steam pressure
   B. the working steam pressure
   C. 1 1/2 times the maximum allowable working pressure
   D. twice the maximum allowable working pressure

23. A disconnected steam pressure gauge is USUALLY calibrated with a(n)

   A. Orsat instrument
   B. air pump
   C. tuyeres
   D. dead-weight tester

24. The recommended size joint for repairing firebrick wall is MOST nearly

   A. 1/64"    B. 1/16"    C. 1/4"    D. 1/2"

25. The acidity of boiler water is USUALLY determined by a _____ test.

   A. Rockwell
   B. soap hardness
   C. paper
   D. alkalinity

26. Electrostatic precipitators are used in power plants to

   A. remove fly ash from flue gases
   B. measure smoke conditions
   C. collect boiler impurities
   D. disperse minerals in feed water

27. Fly ash from the flue gases in a power plant is collected by a

   A. soot blower
   B. gas separator
   C. stack regulator
   D. mechanical separator

4 (#1)

28. The installation of four new split packing rings in a stuffing box requires that the joints of the packing rings be placed _____° apart.

    A. 180　　B. 90　　C. 60　　D. 30

29. In power plants, boiler feed water is chemically treated in order to

    A. prevent scale formation
    B. increase water foaming
    C. increase oxygen formation
    D. increase the temperature of the water

30. The soot in a fire tube boiler GENERALLY settles on the

    A. bridgewall
    B. inside tube surface
    C. combustion chamber sides
    D. outside tube surface

31. The one of the following classifications of fuel oil strainers that is generally NOT used with the heavier industrial fuel oils is a _____ strainer.

    A. wire mesh
    B. metallic disc
    C. filter cloth
    D. perforated metal cylinder

32. The temperature of the fuel oil leaving a pre-heater is controlled by a(n)

    A. potentiometer　　B. relay
    C. low water cut-off　　D. aquastat

33. A pneumatic tool is GENERALLY powered by

    A. natural gas　　B. steam
    C. a battery　　D. air

34. In the city, the maximum steam pressure permitted in the steam coils used for heating the oil in a submerged oil storage tank is MOST NEARLY _____ Psi.

    A. 40　　B. 35　　C. 25　　D. 10

35. The water pressure used in a hydrostatic test on a boiler is GENERALLY _____ maximum working pressure.

    A. 4 times the　　B. 2 times the
    C. 1 1/2 times the　　D. the same as

36. The one of the following valves that should be used in a steam line to throttle the flow is the _____ valve.

    A. plug　　B. check　　C. gate　　D. globe

37. The CO (carbon monoxide) content in the flue gas from an efficiently fired boiler should be APPROXIMATELY

    A. 0% to 1%　　B. 4% to 6%　　C. 8% to 10%　　D. 12% to 13%

38. The $CO_2$ (carbon dioxide) percentage in the flue gas of an efficiently fired boiler should be APPROXIMATELY

    A. 1%  B. 12%  C. 18%  D. 25%

39. When the temperature of stack gases rises considerably above the normal operating stack temperature, it GENERALLY indicates

    A. a low boiler water level
    B. a heavy smoke condition in the stack
    C. that the boiler is operating efficiently
    D. that the boiler tubes are dirty

40. A boiler safety valve is usually set above the maximum working pressure by an amount equal to _____% of the maximum working pressure.

    A. 6  B. 10  C. 12  D. 14

## KEY (CORRECT ANSWERS)

| | | | |
|---|---|---|---|
| 1. A | 11. D | 21. D | 31. C |
| 2. C | 12. A | 22. C | 32. D |
| 3. D | 13. D | 23. D | 33. D |
| 4. B | 14. A | 24. B | 34. D |
| 5. B | 15. C | 25. D | 35. C |
| 6. C | 16. B | 26. A | 36. D |
| 7. D | 17. A | 27. D | 37. A |
| 8. D | 18. A | 28. B | 38. B |
| 9. B | 19. C | 29. A | 39. D |
| 10. A | 20. D | 30. B | 40. A |

# TEST 2

DIRECTIONS: Each question or incomplete statement is followed by several suggested answers or completions. Select the one that BEST answers the question or completes the statement. *PRINT THE LETTER OF THE CORRECT ANSWER IN THE SPACE AT THE RIGHT.*

1. The one of the following grades of fuel oil that contains the GREATEST heating value, in BTU per gallon, is

    A. #2  B. #4  C. #5  D. #6

    1._____

2. When we say that a fuel oil has a high viscosity, we mean MAINLY that the fuel oil will

    A. evaporate easily
    B. burn without smoke
    C. flow slowly through pipes
    D. have a low specific gravity

    2._____

3. The type of fuel oil pump GENERALLY used with a rotary cup oil burner system is the _____ pump.

    A. propeller           B. internal
    C. centrifugal         D. piston

    3._____

4. No. 6 fuel oil flowing to a mechanical atomizing burner should be preheated to APPROXIMATELY _____ ° F.

    A. 185  B. 115  C. 100  D. 80

    4._____

5. The flame of an industrial rotary cup oil burner should be adjusted so that the flame

    A. has a yellow color with blue spots
    B. strikes all sides of the combustion chamber
    C. has a light brown color
    D. does not strike the rear of the combustion chamber

    5._____

6. The location of the oil burner *remote control switch* should GENERALLY be

    A. at the boiler room entrance
    B. on the boiler shell
    C. on the oil burner motor
    D. on a wall nearest the boiler

    6._____

7. With forced draft, the approximate wind box pressure in a single-retort underfeed stoker is NORMALLY

    A. 2"  B. 5"  C. 7"  D. 9"

    7._____

8. The pressure over the fire in a coal-fired steam boiler with a balanced-draft system and natural draft is MOST NEARLY

    A. +.60"  B. +.50"  C. -.02"  D. -.70"

    8._____

9. Three tons of coal with an ash content of 10% will yield a weight of ash of MOST NEARLY _____ pounds.

   A. 400  B. 500  C. 600  D. 700

10. To clean and spread the coal over the grates of a coal-fired boiler, a stationary fireman would use a tool known as a(n)

    A. hoe
    B. extractor
    C. lance
    D. slice bar

11. To burn the volatile matter in coal more efficiently, one should

    A. mix peat with the coal
    B. supply overfire draft
    C. mix it with a lower grade of coal
    D. add moisture to the coal

12. The one of the following that lists the size classifications of anthracite coal in proper order ranging from the smallest to the largest is

    A. chestnut, culm, pea, birdseye, egg
    B. egg, stove, pea, broken, culm
    C. stove, egg, birdseye, culm, broken
    D. birdseye, pea, chestnut, stove, egg

13. The fire in a hand-fired furnace can be cleaned by a method known as

    A. ashpit to grate
    B. bottom to top
    C. side to side
    D. grate to crown

14. Coal is normally *tempered* when operating a chain-grate stoker for the purpose of

    A. increasing coking
    B. preventing clinking
    C. collecting particles
    D. promoting uniform burning

15. The one of the following coals that can legally be burned in city power plants is

    A. anthracite
    B. sub-bituminous
    C. non-coking
    D. bituminous

16. The one of the following that is known as *rice coal* is

    A. pea coal
    B. buckwheat (No. 2 coal)
    C. egg coal
    D. culm coal

17. A MAJOR cause of air pollution resulting from the burning of fuel oils is _____ dioxide.

    A. sulphur  B. silicon  C. nitrous  D. hydrogen

18. The $CO_2$ percentage in the flue gas of a power plant is indicated by a

    A. Doppler meter
    B. Ranarex indicator
    C. Microtector
    D. hygrometer

19. The MOST likely cause of black smoke exhausting from the chimney of an oil-fired boiler is    19.____

    A. high secondary air flow   B. low stack emission
    C. low oil temperature        D. high chimney draft

20. The diameter of the steam piston in a steam-driven duplex vacuum pump whose dimensions are given as 3 by 2 by 4 is    20.____

    A. 2    B. 3    C. 4    D. 6

21. An induced draft fan is GENERALLY connected between the    21.____

    A. condenser and the first pass
    B. stack and the breeching
    C. feedwater heater and the boiler feed pump
    D. combustion chamber and fuel oil tanks

22. The purpose of an air chamber on a reciprocating water pump is to    22.____

    A. maintain a uniform flow
    B. reduce the amount of steam expansion
    C. create a pulsating flow
    D. vary the amount of steam admission

23. *Flash point* is the temperature at which oil will    23.____

    A. change completely to vapor
    B. safely fire in a furnace
    C. flash into flame if a lighted match is passed just above the top of the oil
    D. burn intermittently when ignited

24. A *sounding box* would NORMALLY be found    24.____

    A. on top of the boiler
    B. next to a compressed air tank
    C. in a fuel oil tank
    D. in a steam condenser

25. An *intercooler* is GENERALLY found on a(n)    25.____

    A. steam pump      B. air compressor
    C. steam engine    D. rotary oil pump

26. The instrument used to measure atmospheric pressure is a    26.____

    A. capillary tube    B. venturi
    C. barometer         D. calorimeter

27. The control which starts or stops the operation of the oil burner at a predetermined steam pressure is the    27.____

    A. pressuretrol      B. air flow interlock
    C. transformer       D. magnetic oil valve

28. In a closed feedwater heater, the water and the steam       28.____

    A. come into direct contact
    B. are kept apart from each other
    C. are under negative pressure
    D. mix and exhaust to the atmosphere

29. A *knocking* noise in steam lines is GENERALLY the result of       29.____

    A. superheated steam expansion
    B. high steam pressure
    C. condensation in the line
    D. rapid steam expansion

30. An electrical component known as a step-up transformer operates by       30.____

    A. raising voltage and decreasing amperage
    B. decreasing amperage and raising resistance
    C. raising amperage and decreasing resistance
    D. raising voltage and amperage at the same time

31. A manometer is an instrument that is used to measure       31.____

    A. heat radiation              B. air volume
    C. condensate water level      D. air pressure

32. Three 75-gallon per hour mechanical pressure type oil burners operating together are to burn 150,000 gallons of No. 6 fuel oil.       32.____
    The number of hours they would take to burn this amount of oil is MOST NEARLY

    A. 665        B. 760        C. 870        D. 1210

33. The sum of 10 1/2, 8 3/4, 5 1/2, and 2 1/2 is       33.____

    A. 23         B. 25         C. 26         D. 27

34. A water tank measures 50 feet long, 16 feet wide, and 12 feet high. Assume that water weighs 60 pounds per cubic foot and that one gallon of water weighs 8 pounds. The number of gallons the tank can hold when it is half full is       34.____

    A. 21,500     B. 28,375     C. 33,410     D. 36,000

35. Assuming 70 gallons of oil cost $42.00, then 110 gallons of oil at the same rate will cost       35.____

    A. $66.00     B. $84.00     C. $96.00     D. $152.00

Questions 36-40.

DIRECTIONS: Questions 36 through 40 are to be answered on the basis of the information contained in the following paragraph.

Fuel is conserved when a boiler is operating near its most efficient load. The efficiency of a boiler will change as the output varies. Large amounts of air must be used at low ratings and so the heat exchanger is inefficient. As the output increases, the efficiency decreases due to an increase in flue gas temperature. Every boiler has an output rate for which its efficiency is highest. For example, in a water-tube boiler, the highest efficiency might occur at

120 percent of rated capacity while in a vertical fire-tube boiler highest efficiency might be at 70% of rated capacity.

The type of fuel burned and cleanliness affect the maximum efficiency of the boiler. When a power plant contains a battery of boilers, a sufficient number should be kept in operation so as to maintain the output of individual units near their points of maximum efficiency. One of the boilers in the battery can be used as a regulator to meet the change in demand for steam while the other boilers could still operate at their most efficient rating. Boiler performance is expressed as the number of pounds of steam generated per pound of fuel.

36. According to the above paragraph, the number of pounds of steam generated per pound of fuel is a measure of boiler

    A. size
    B. performance
    C. regulator input
    D. by-pass

37. According to the above paragraph, the HIGHEST efficiency of a vertical fire-tube boiler might occur at _____ capacity.

    A. 70% of rated
    B. 80% of water tube
    C. 95% of water tube
    D. 120% of rated

38. According to the above paragraph, the MAXIMUM efficiency of a boiler is affected by

    A. atmospheric temperature
    B. atmospheric pressure
    C. cleanliness
    D. fire brick material

39. According to the above paragraph, a heat exchanger uses large amounts of air at low

    A. fuel rates
    B. ratings
    C. temperatures
    D. pressures

40. According to the above paragraph, one boiler in a battery of boilers should be used as a

    A. demand    B. stand-by    C. regulator    D. safety

## KEY (CORRECT ANSWERS)

| | | | | | | | |
|---|---|---|---|---|---|---|---|
| 1. | D | 11. | B | 21. | B | 31. | D |
| 2. | C | 12. | D | 22. | A | 32. | A |
| 3. | C | 13. | C | 23. | B | 33. | D |
| 4. | A | 14. | D | 24. | C | 34. | D |
| 5. | D | 15. | A | 25. | B | 35. | A |
| 6. | A | 16. | B | 26. | C | 36. | B |
| 7. | A | 17. | A | 27. | A | 37. | A |
| 8. | C | 18. | B | 28. | B | 38. | C |
| 9. | C | 19. | C | 29. | C | 39. | B |
| 10. | A | 20. | B | 30. | A | 40. | C |

# EXAMINATION SECTION
## TEST 1

DIRECTIONS: Each question or incomplete statement is followed by several suggested answers or completions. Select the one that BEST answers the question or completes the statement. *PRINT THE LETTER OF THE CORRECT ANSWER IN THE SPACE AT THE RIGHT.*

1. A(n) _____ pump is used to transfer fuel oil.  1._____

    A. gear
    B. injector
    C. centrifugal
    D. reciprocating

2. A fuel oil tank is located above the pump. A siphon should be located between the  2._____

    A. preheater and pump
    B. pump and boiler
    C. tank and pump
    D. tank and aquastat

3. *WOG* stands for  3._____

    A. water or gas
    B. water, oil, gas
    C. water, gas, steam
    D. all of the above

4. The _____ pump is NOT a positive displacement pump.  4._____

    A. gear
    B. centrifugal
    C. screw
    D. reciprocating

5. An unloader is used on an air compressor to  5._____

    A. start easier
    B. stop easier
    C. run faster
    D. none of the above

6. An intercooler is associated with a(n)  6._____

    A. air compressor
    B. steam engine
    C. feedwater heater
    D. condenser

7. What is added to oil to prevent sludge or lacquer from forming?  7._____

    A. Detergents
    B. Anti-foaming agents
    C. Inhibitors
    D. Phosphates

8. Greatest wear occurs on a steam turbine between the moving and stationary parts  8._____

    A. at 20% over normal speed
    B. at 10% over normal speed
    C. at normal speed
    D. below normal speed

9. A *gag* is USUALLY put on a safety prior to  9._____

    A. external inspection
    B. internal inspection
    C. hydrostatic inspection
    D. removing hand holes

10. To calibrate a steam gauge, you use a  10._____

    A. dead weight tester
    B. fyrite instrument
    C. spring scale lifter
    D. pyrometer

11. When not more than two safety valves of different sizes are used, the relieving capacity of the smaller valve shall NOT be less than _____ % of the larger valve.

    A. 20  B. 30  C. 40  D. 50

12. *Blow off* piping USUALLY refers to

    A. piping at the lowest part of the boiler
    B. piping coming from the safeties
    C. piping coming from the superheater
    D. vent pipes

13. The heating value of coal is 14,000 BTU per pound. It is necessary to produce 1,400,000 BTU per hour.
    If a boiler has a 60% efficiency rate, how many pounds must be burned?

    A. 60  B. 170  C. 225  D. 100

14. You are working the 4:00 P.M. to Midnight shift at an energy producing, coal burning steam plant.
    The FIRST thing you would do when coming to work is

    A. add green coal and build up the fire
    B. blow down gauge glass and determine water level
    C. clean the fires
    D. blow down the boiler

15. On a 3" safety valve set to blow at 300 psi, what is the pressure needed to lift it?

    A. 2120  B. 300  C. 3000  D. 2425

16. On a horizontal return tubular boiler, there is a baffle located near the exit of the boiler. Its purpose is to provide _____ steam.

    A. wet
    B. dry
    C. superheated
    D. saturated

17. Most high temperature, high pressure boilers have high evaporative rates.
    Because of this,

    A. water must be treated so that scale does not form on the inside of the tubes
    B. it maintains proper water levels
    C. it operates efficiently
    D. it works better with no returns

18. Soot is formed on a water tube boiler

    A. on the fan blades of the forced draft fan
    B. on the inside of the tubes
    C. on the outside of the tubes
    D. in the steam drum

19. In order to make a tight joint between a tube and a tube sheet,

    A. use a self-feeding tube expander
    B. use a ball-peen hammer and a blunt cold chisel
    C. weld in place
    D. heat will expand the tubes

20. Give external heating area in square feet of tube with the following dimensions: tube interior diameter, 5 inches; wall thickness, 1/2 inch and 18 feet long.

    A. 19.25    B. 24.25    C. 26.50    D. 28.26

21. Give external heating area in square feet of 100 tubes 3 1/2 inches external diameter, 12 feet long.

    A. 1100    B. 1200    C. 1300    D. 1400

22. A safety valve capacity must be such that it can discharge all the steam that a boiler can generate without rising more than _____% above the highest pressure at which any safety valve is set.

    A. 3    B. 6    C. 7    D. 8

23. The depth of the fuel bed on a chain grate stoker is controlled by a

    A. guillotine or knife gate
    B. height of ignition arch
    C. speed of stoker drive or air pressure
    D. size of grates

24. Tuyeres are used to provide air for

    A. an underfed stoker            B. a sprinkler stoker
    C. a rotary cup burner           D. steam atomizing burners

25. A pulverized boiler has the GREATEST danger of explosion when it has a _____ rate of fire.

    A. low    B. 70%    C. 100%    D. 110%

# KEY (CORRECT ANSWERS)

| | | | |
|---|---|---|---|
| 1. | A | 11. | D |
| 2. | C | 12. | A |
| 3. | B | 13. | B |
| 4. | B | 14. | B |
| 5. | A | 15. | A |
| 6. | A | 16. | B |
| 7. | A | 17. | A |
| 8. | D | 18. | C |
| 9. | C | 19. | A |
| 10. | A | 20. | D |

21. A
22. B
23. A
24. A
25. A

# TEST 2

DIRECTIONS: Each question or incomplete statement is followed by several suggested answers or completions. Select the one that BEST answers the question or completes the statement. *PRINT THE LETTER OF THE CORRECT ANSWER IN THE SPACE AT THE RIGHT.*

1. Draft is measured in

    A. pounds per square inch
    B. inches of mercury
    C. feet of water
    D. inches of water

    1.____

2. In a natural draft boiler, a _____ is used to prevent excess draft from occurring.

    A. siphon
    B. stack switch
    C. barometric damper
    D. all of the above

    2.____

3. Approximate analysis would include

    A. fixed carbon, moisture, and ash
    B. sulphur, volatile matter, and moisture
    C. ash, moisture, volatile matter, and fixed carbon,
    D. fixed carbon, ash, and volatile matter

    3.____

4. What is considered good combustion in an oil-fired boiler? _____% $CO_2$.

    A. 8
    B. 10
    C. 12
    D. 14

    4.____

5. In an oil-fired boiler, the flue gas analysis indicates 10.5% $CO_2$. This would indicate an excess air of MOST NEARLY

    A. 30%
    B. 40%
    C. 60%
    D. 70%

    5.____

6. In terms of environmental pollution, the three elements which are MOST damaging are

    A. carbon monoxide, sulphur, and particulate matter
    B. carbon dioxide, sulphur, and oxygen
    C. particulate matter, sulphur, and carbon dioxide
    D. oxygen and sulphur

    6.____

7. A rotary cup burner is easy to distinguish because it has a(n)

    A. oil line and steam line
    B. high pressure air line and low pressure air line
    C. oil line and centrifugal fan
    D. oil line, air line, and steam line

    7.____

8. What type of fire extinguisher would be used on a *live* electrical wire?

    A. Soda foam
    B. Water
    C. Carbon dioxide
    D. Halon

    8.____

9. Fuel oil is heated in a storage tank by use of

    A. fuel oil burner
    B. steam
    C. hot air
    D. electric coils

    9.____

73

10. The LOWEST point at which fuel oil will flow under standard conditions is known as

    A. viscosity point   B. flashpoint
    C. pour point        D. specific gravity

11. What lubrication would you NOT use when the temperature was 160°?

    A. Calcium   B. Sodium   C. Lithium   D. Aluminum

12. To lubricate the piston on the water end of a duplex pump, you would use

    A. water   B. oil   C. grease   D. graphite

13. To oil multiple bearings in an enclosed space, use a

    A. ring or chain oiler   B. drip
    C. splash                D. capillary

14. A new boiler is erected and the main supports are from the roof.
    An advantage of this method is

    A. to relieve pressure at the bottom of the boiler
    B. to allow for expansion
    C. it is easier to build
    D. it is less expensive

15. How many cubic feet are there in a coal bin that is 24 feet long and 20 feet wide if the front of the bin is 4 feet high and the rear of the bin is 12 feet high?

    A. 4000   B. 6000   C. 2000   D. 8000

16. The purpose of a feedwater heater used with a boiler is to heat

    A. and treat water used in the boiler
    B. the fuel oil
    C. the steam
    D. the intake air

17. On a d-slide valve engine, lengthening the valve stem causes earlier

    A. crank-end admission   B. head-end admission
    C. crank-end cutoff      D. head-end compression

18. The dimensions of a pump are 18 x 16 x 24. What does 16 stand for?

    A. Steam end          B. Water end
    C. Valve stem length  D. Steam flow

19. A centrifugal pump makes more noise as the rate of water pressure increases.
    The reason for this is

    A. specific gravity of water
    B. cavitation
    C. the water is too hot
    D. none of the above

20. Which of the following is NOT a positive displacement pump?

    A. Screw type   B. Reciprocating   C. Gear type   D. Centrifugal

21. An injector is the same as a(n)   21.____

   A. ejector
   B. boiler feed pump
   C. tank
   D. blow down tank

22. A closed feedwater heater has steam   22.____

   A. going through the feedwater heater
   B. and water mixing directly
   C. and water not in direct contact
   D. and air mixing together

23. M.E.P. stands for   23.____

   A. minimum exhaust pressure
   B. maximum efficiency point
   C. mean effective pressure
   D. maximum exhaust pressure

24. The MAIN function of the steam jacket in a steam engine is to   24.____

   A. *reduce* initial condensation in the cylinders
   B. *decrease* the superheat of the steam going to the cylinders
   C. *increase* the expansion of steam in the cylinders
   D. *decrease* the speed of the engine

25. In a noncondensing steam engine, the compounding reduces the steam consumption by   25.____

   A. 5% to 10%   B. 10 to 25%   C. 25 to 40%   D. 40 to 50%

---

# KEY (CORRECT ANSWERS)

| | | | |
|---|---|---|---|
| 1. D | | 11. D | |
| 2. C | | 12. A | |
| 3. C | | 13. A | |
| 4. C | | 14. B | |
| 5. B | | 15. A | |
| 6. A | | 16. A | |
| 7. C | | 17. A | |
| 8. C | | 18. B | |
| 9. B | | 19. D | |
| 10. C | | 20. D | |

21. B
22. C
23. C
24. A
25. C

# TEST 3

DIRECTIONS: Each question or incomplete statement is followed by several suggested answers or completions. Select the one that BEST answers the question or completes the statement. *PRINT THE LETTER OF THE CORRECT ANSWER IN THE SPACE AT THE RIGHT.*

1. The steam rate on a steam engine can be expressed as

   A. degrees Fahrenheit
   B. per pound of fuel burned
   C. pounds per hour
   D. gallons of water

2. In a steam generating plant operating condensing, if a deaerating heater is used, it would be located between the

   A. boiler and condenser on the feedwater line
   B. boiler and the condenser on the exhaust line
   C. engine and the condenser on the exhaust line
   D. engine and the condenser on the main steam line

3. A manufacturing plant is equipped with a bleeder turbine with the bleed steam used for the purpose of processing. When the demand for process steam falls off, the bled steam is

   A. exhausted into the atmosphere
   B. put into the heating system
   C. used in the lower pressure stages of the turbine
   D. all of the above

4. A turbine generator at full load runs at 1765 RPM. At no load, it runs at 1800 RPM. Its speed regulation is MOST NEARLY

   A. 2%     B. 3%     C. 5%     D. 10%

5. _____ are NOT used to seal the steam space of a turbine.

   A. Labyrinth seals          B. Carbon packing rings
   C. Water glands             D. Oil seals

6. A motor with a large starting torque is a _____ motor.

   A. squirrel cage induction   B. synchronous
   C. shunt wound               D. wound induction

7. What is the horsepower of an engine having an 8 x 12 cylinder, mean effective pressure of 90, and an RPM of 330?

   A. 50     B. 90     C. 100     D. 190

8. You get oil out of boiler feedwater by

   A. deionization             B. coagulation
   C. lime-soda process        D. absorbal process

9. How many poles does a 60 frequency, 1200 RPM motor have?  9.____

   A. 4   B. 6   C. 8   D. 10

10. A 3 phase, 4 wire distribution panel, having a line to line voltage of 208 volts, has a line to  10.____
    neutral of MOST NEARLY _____ volts.

    A. 208   B. 150   C. 120   D. 24

11. After a boiler is inspected, a notice is given to the owner.  11.____
    This should be posted

    A. on the door
    B. in the bathroom
    C. near the boiler
    D. in the owner's apartment or house

12. The MINIMUM diameter of a boiler safety is _____ inch.  12.____

    A. 3/4   B. 1/2   C. 1   D. 1 1/4

13. The MAXIMUM diameter of a boiler safety is _____ inches.  13.____

    A. 44   B. 4   C. 3 1/2   D. 3

14. On stoker fired boilers with gas ignition, the MAXIMUM flow of gas per minute is  14.____

    A. 1000   B. 1500   C. 200   D. 1500

15. On gas boilers producing over 400,000 BTU's per hour, the gas will be terminated if there  15.____
    is no flame detected for a period of _____ seconds.

    A. 2   B. 3   C. 4   D. 10

16. What is the MINIMUM thickness on steel plated boilers?  16.____
    _____ inch.

    A. 1/4   B. 1/2   C. 5/8   D. 7/8

17. What is the MINIMUM thickness on cast iron boilers?  17.____
    _____ inch.

    A. 1/4   B. 1/2   C. 5/8   D. 7/8

18. On a safety valve, there is a device that will lift the valve off the seat (without pressure) a  18.____
    MINIMUM of _____ inch.

    A. 1/16   B. 1/8   C. 1/4   D. 1/2

19. If a boiler in a battery can be disconnected, what kind of valve must be on the conden-  19.____
    sate return line?

    A. Angle   B. Globe   C. Gate   D. Check

20. The siphon on a steam gauge shall have a MINIMUM diameter of _____ inch.  20.____

    A. 1/4   B. 3/8   C. 1/2   D. 3/4

21. Hot water boilers in multiple dwellings do NOT have to be inspected if there are fewer than _____ families.

    A. 2  B. 6  C. 8  D. 10

22. The pressure gauge on a boiler shall show steam pressure

    A. 15% over steam pressure
    B. 1 1/2 times over steam pressure
    C. 2 times over steam pressure
    D. not less than 30 psig

23. The boiler will automatically shut down if the steam pressure is _____ percent over the maximum.

    A. 1  B. 2  C. 3  D. 5

24. On a gas boiler, how long does the pre-ignition period last before lighting off? _____ seconds.

    A. 30  B. 60  C. 90  D. 120

25. In an oil fired boiler using 3 gallons of oil an hour, how much time will lapse when there is no fire before the fuel supply stops? _____ seconds.

    A. 60  B. 120  C. 90  D. 30

## KEY (CORRECT ANSWERS)

| | | | |
|---|---|---|---|
| 1. C | | 11. C | |
| 2. C | | 12. A | |
| 3. A | | 13. A | |
| 4. A | | 14. A | |
| 5. D | | 15. C | |
| 6. A | | 16. A | |
| 7. B | | 17. C | |
| 8. B | | 18. A | |
| 9. B | | 19. C | |
| 10. C | | 20. A | |

21. B
22. D
23. D
24. A
25. C

# EXAMINATION SECTION
# TEST 1

DIRECTIONS: Each question or incomplete statement is followed by several suggested answers or completions. Select the one that BEST answers the question or completes the statement. *PRINT THE LETTER OF THE CORRECT ANSWER IN THE SPACE AT THE RIGHT.*

1. What type of condenser would you install to conserve water?

    A. Shell and tube
    B. Evaporative
    C. Atmospheric
    D. Double pipe

2. The engine room first aid kit should contain _____ acid.

    A. hydrochloric
    B. nitric
    C. sulphuric
    D. picric

3. The steam jet refrigeration system is used for

    A. deep freezing work
    B. air conditioning work
    C. cold storage
    D. the noon whistle

4. A flooded evaporator USUALLY has a(n) _____ metering device.

    A. high side float
    B. low side float
    C. automatic expansion valve
    D. thermostatic expansion valve

5. Refrigerant enters the condenser as a _____ and leaves as a _____.

    A. high pressure gas; high pressure liquid
    B. high pressure gas; low pressure liquid
    C. high pressure liquid; low pressure liquid
    D. superheated gas; superheated gas

6. When a high side float is punctured and sinks, it results in

    A. starved evaporator
    B. flooded evaporator
    C. frozen valve
    D. high head pressure

7. A compound gauge registers

    A. inches of pressure present
    B. pounds of pressure below atmospheric pressure
    C. inches of water above atmosphere and inches of air below
    D. pounds of pressure above atmosphere and inches of vacuum below

8. An air conditioning Freon compressor is equipped with a unit shell and coil condenser-receiver slung under the base of the compressor.
   If the system is overcharged with refrigerant, the PROBABILITY is that

    A. only head pressure would go up
    B. both head pressure and suction pressure would go up
    C. capacity of the compressor would go up
    D. system would continue to operate without change

9. In relation to compressors, which statement is MOST correct?

   A. Valve lift for low speed reciprocating compressors is less.
   B. The HP per ton decreases as the suction decreases.
   C. The refrigerating effect per pound of refrigerant decreases as the suction pressure increases.
   D. The valve lift for high speed reciprocating compressors should be less than required for low speed compressors.

10. What type of constant speed motor is generally used in large refrigerating plants?

    A. Slip ring
    B. Synchronous
    C. Squirrel gauge
    D. Double wound squirrel gauge

11. The capacity of an evaporative condenser will INCREASE if the

    A. wet bulb reading is high
    B. wet bulb reading is low
    C. capacity does not change
    D. amount of water used is less

12. One ton of refrigeration is equal to how many BTUs?

    A. 1,200 per minute         B. 200 per hour
    C. 12,000 per hour          D. 288,000 per hour

13. A(n) _____ condenser could be used in winter without water.

    A. submerged                B. shell and tube
    C. shell and coil           D. atmospheric with drip

14. The evaporative coils in a cooler are along the ceiling, and one of these coils has insulating baffles.
    The baffles are there to

    A. catch the dripping when the coils are defrosting
    B. supply gravity air to circulate in the cooler
    C. see that gravity air circulates over the coils
    D. none of the above

15. In methyl chloride systems, a dryer would PROBABLY be placed in the _____ near the _____.

    A. discharge; compressor
    B. liquid line; expansion valve
    C. suction line; compressor
    D. suction line; evaporator

16. A Freon 12 compressor used in an air conditioning system has a magnetic bypass to

    A. equalize pressure in the cylinder
    B. relieve pressure when it becomes high
    C. regulate compressor capacity
    D. relieve oil from the cylinder to the crankcase

17. The formula $C = 0.8P_1D^2$ is used for determining the capacity of a

    A. fusible plug
    B. stop valve
    C. safety valve
    D. venturi

18. A scale trap is placed in the suction line of a compression system to remove foreign matter. It would be MOST effective when the plant is

    A. new
    B. shut down for a long time
    C. old
    D. none of the above

19. In a small ammonia plant using brine as a cooling agent, due to a leak, the brine became saturated with ammonia. After fixing the leak, you, as an operator, would

    A. dump the brine and make up a new batch
    B. recirculate the brine through the system; if no leaks, reuse it
    C. treat the brine with Nessler's solution and reuse it
    D. treat the brine with sulphur and reuse it

20. When starting a large air conditioning system of the reciprocating type on a day when the latent heat load is high, one of the FIRST things an engineer should do is

    A. open the bypass valve to lighten the load
    B. set the thermostat a few degrees higher
    C. install larger fuses to take the starting load
    D. turn on the cooling water and start the air blower

21. Which of the following statements is CORRECT?
    A(n)

    A. enclosed cooling tower has a forced draft effect
    B. spray pond works exactly like an evaporative condenser
    C. evaporative condenser depends upon the evaporation of some water for its economical operation
    D. evaporative condenser has no refrigerant coil in it

22. The symbol for refrigeration shown at the right represents

    A. high side float
    B. low side float
    C. water valve
    D. oil trap

23. The one of the following types of condensers in which eliminator plates are USUALLY found is the _____ type

    A. shell and coil
    B. shell and tube
    C. evaporative
    D. double tube

24. There are several test cocks on a Freon receiver condenser. The one at the end, about one quarter of the way up from the bottom. This test cock is used for

    A. purging non-condensable gases or air from the system
    B. testing the liquid level in the receiver
    C. an auxiliary charging connection
    D. pumping down purposes

25. The FASTEST way to remove the frost from direct expansion coils in a cold storage room is to

    A. spray water over them
    B. shut the coils off and let the frost melt off
    C. chop or scrape the frost off
    D. run a hot gas line to the coils

---

# KEY (CORRECT ANSWERS)

| | | | |
|---|---|---|---|
| 1. B | | 11. B | |
| 2. D | | 12. C | |
| 3. B | | 13. D | |
| 4. B | | 14. C | |
| 5. A | | 15. B | |
| 6. A | | 16. C | |
| 7. D | | 17. A | |
| 8. B | | 18. A | |
| 9. D | | 19. A | |
| 10. B | | 20. D | |

21. C
22. A
23. C
24. B
25. D

# TEST 2

DIRECTIONS: Each question or incomplete statement is followed by several suggested answers or completions. Select the one that BEST answers the question or completes the statement. *PRINT THE LETTER OF THE CORRECT ANSWER IN THE SPACE AT THE RIGHT.*

1. In a shell and tube brine cooler with an electric float valve, if the gas equalizer line is clogged,

    A. it operates normally
    B. liquid in the tank goes up and down
    C. liquid in the tank does not correspond with the level in the float
    D. there is no change

1.____

2. The weak liquor heat exchanger or an ammonia absorption system is used to pre-

    A. heat weak liquor
    B. heat strong liquor
    C. cool strong liquor
    D. cool suction gas

2.____

3. The subcooling of liquid refrigerant, immediately before the liquid passes through the expansion valve, would MOST likely result in an increase

    A. of 50% in the horsepower per ton factor
    B. in head pressure
    C. in compressor speed
    D. in the net available refrigerating effect

3.____

4. A Freon compressor was V-belt driven when installed, but the belts were too tight. After the unit has been running for a while, this will

    A. increase the speed of the compressor
    B. decrease the speed of the motor and the compressor
    C. increase the speed of the motor
    D. cause the motor to run hot

4.____

5. In a room, there is a cylinder half-filled with ammonia at 50° F. The pressure inside the tank will be _____ pounds.

    A. 40    B. 125    C. 75    D. 250

5.____

6. What percentage of oil travels with refrigerant in a system?

    A. 10%    B. 125%    C. 30%    D. 50%

6.____

7. When attempting to read the high side pressure gauge on an operating ammonia compressor, it is noted that the pointer *hunts,* or has a wide and relatively slow back and forth movement. This would MOST likely indicate that the compressor

    A. is overloaded
    B. valve action is sluggish
    C. suction valves are stuck
    D. is operating normally

7.____

8. One DISADVANTAGE of using carbon dioxide is that it has a lower critical point than usual, close to _____ ° F.

    A. 67    B. 144    C. 39.4    D. 87

8.____

9. If a Freon 12 single-acting compressor had oil foaming in the crankcase, this would be caused by

   A. addition of liquid Freon
   B. sudden drop in oil temperature
   C. addition of oil to the crankcase
   D. sudden drop in crankcase pressure

10. The refrigerant that separates from the lubricating oil in an operating evaporator with oil floating on top of the liquid refrigerant is

    A. Freon 12
    B. Freon 22
    C. ammonia
    D. carbon dioxide

11. In a system using a silica gel drier that has picked up moisture, it may be reactivated by heating it for a period of four hours or more, at a temperature of APPROXIMATELY _____ °F.

    A. 200
    B. 700
    C. 450
    D. 850

12. In a large plant, there are several squirrel gauge motors and three or four synchronous motors.
    One purpose of the synchronous motor is

    A. to correct the power factor
    B. to correct the plant power demand
    C. to allow for more than one speed
    D. its high speed

13. Of the different types of solenoid valves used in refrigeration, the one which, when energized, tends to close the port is the _____ type.

    A. closed
    B. normally open
    C. fluctuating
    D. partially closed

14. A Freon 12 compressor used for air conditioning has a low temperature cooling coil of 45° (no superheat).
    The low temperature gas coming back to the compressor would be

    A. 20#
    B. 40#
    C. 60#
    D. 80#

15. In a given temperature of air, the ratio of vapor pressure to humidity is called

    A. absolute humidity
    B. relative humidity
    C. pressure
    D. partial pressure

16. A compressor that has two compression strokes and two suction strokes per cylinder per revolution of the crankshaft is a

    A. single-acting compressor
    B. double-acting compressor
    C. two stage compressor
    D. compressor in duplex

17. In the lubrication of a Freon refrigeration compressor,   17._____

    A. vegetable oil is preferred for best results
    B. Freon has the same degree of miscibility with oils as does ammonia
    C. a chemical action between the Freon and lubricating oil occurs
    D. the refrigerant mixes with the lubricating oil

18. The refrigerant stored in a machinery room shall NOT be more than _____% of the normal charge or more than _____ pounds of refrigerant in addition to the charge in the system.   18._____

    A. 20; 300     B. 30; 300     C. 35; 350     D. 25; 325

19. A motor has a protection device to prevent burning out or damage called a   19._____

    A. fusetron              B. dual fuse
    C. circuit breaker       D. thermal protector

20. For a pressure testing of newly installed R-12 systems, it is BEST to use   20._____

    A. dry carbon dioxide with a trace of R-12 in it
    B. water in a hydrostatic test
    C. dry hydrogen with a trace of R-12 in it
    D. anhydrous ammonia

21. A dehydrator should be used in a(n) _____ system.   21._____

    A. sulphur dioxide       B. Freon 12
    C. ammonia               D. carbon dioxide

22. In the absorption system, the flow of ammonia gas in relation to the strong liquor in the analyzer is _____ flow.   22._____

    A. cross     B. counter     C. parallel     D. diagonal

23. A volume of water of 10,000 cubic inches weighs _____ pounds.   23._____

    A. 144     B. 970     C. 361     D. 231

24. The refrigerant known as *Refrigerant 40* is   24._____

    A. propane              B. sulphur dioxide
    C. methyl chloride      D. ammonia

25. What design of valve would you use for an expansion valve?   25._____
    A _____ valve.

    A. globe     B. needle
    C. gate      D. V-notched globe

# KEY (CORRECT ANSWERS)

1. C
2. B
3. D
4. D
5. C

6. A
7. B
8. D
9. D
10. D

11. C
12. A
13. B
14. B
15. B

16. B
17. D
18. A
19. D
20. A

21. B
22. B
23. C
24. C
25. B

---

# TEST 3

DIRECTIONS: Each question or incomplete statement is followed by several suggested answers or completions. Select the one that BEST answers the question or completes the statement. *PRINT THE LETTER OF THE CORRECT ANSWER IN THE SPACE AT THE RIGHT.*

1. In comparing the absorption system with the compression system, the steam coil in the generator is equivalent to the    1.____

    A. hot discharge refrigerant vapor
    B. electric motor
    C. hot discharge valve assembly
    D. compressor

2. On a horizontal compressor having a gravity feed oil system from a tank above the compressor, the pressure inside the tank is    2.____

    A. zero psig
    B. 14.7 gauge
    C. 20 pounds
    D. 10 pounds above suction

3. Which of the following would cause frost to form on the outer surface of an evaporator coil?    3.____

    A. Water in the refrigerant
    B. Water in the liquid line
    C. Moisture in the refrigerant
    D. Moisture in the air within the cooler

4. The material used for the packing of an ammonia stuffing box would MOST likely be    4.____

    A. steel
    B. solid lead
    C. bellows and spring arrangement
    D. graphite, hemp, and lead

5. It is CORRECT to state that    5.____

    A. copper cannot be used with R-12
    B. aluminum cannot be used with methyl chloride
    C. black iron cannot be used with R-22
    D. magnesium can be used with Freon

6. What color does blue litmus paper turn when ammonia is present?    6.____

    A. Red
    B. White
    C. Green
    D. None of the above

7. In the absorption system, the condenser, receiver, expansion valve, and the evaporator can be designed    7.____

    A. similar to the compression equipment
    B. as an open type design

C. the same as the compression equipment, only zinc coated
D. of copper only

8. You would NOT use muntz metal with

   A. carbon dioxide
   B. Freon 12
   C. ammonia
   D. methyl chloride

   8.____

9. A ten-ton refrigeration unit has the capacity of _____ BTU per minute.

   A. 2,000     B. 20,000     C. 12,000     D. 288,000

   9.____

10. The oil gauge pressure on an ammonia vertical compressor should be

    A. zero pounds when the suction pressure is zero per inch
    B. forty pounds
    C. 30 psig when the suction pressure is 10 psig
    D. 50 pounds fluctuating with the discharge pressure

    10.____

11. The MINIMUM required rated discharge capacity of a pressure relief device or fusible plug for a refrigerant-containing vessel, shall be determined by the formula C = Fdl. C is equal to

    A. feet per second
    B. feet per hour
    C. refrigerant per ton
    D. air in # per minute

    11.____

12. What percentage of oil is mixed with the refrigerant in the compression cycle?

    A. 10%     B. 20%     C. 30%     D. 40%

    12.____

13. If the liquid line were *warmer* than usual, it would indicate

    A. excessive refrigerant
    B. shortage of refrigerant
    C. receiver full of liquid
    D. high head pressure

    13.____

14. A spare rupture member can be substituted for a relief valve in a(n) _____ system.

    A. aqua ammonia
    B. sulphur dioxide
    C. carbon dioxide
    D. ammonia

    14.____

15. What kind of piping would you NOT choose for anhydrous ammonia or aqua ammonia?

    A. Black steel
    B. Stainless steel
    C. Galvanized steel
    D. Wrought iron

    15.____

16. In an absorption system, if the heat exchanger were removed, the result would be to

    A. more steam added to the generator to get results
    B. stop the liquid pump from the absorber
    C. stop the weak liquor pump from the generator
    D. pipe the cold gas from the evaporator directly to the generator

    16.____

17. What produces the LOWER reading of the wet bulb?

    A. The thermometer is calibrated that way
    B. Cooling by evaporation
    C. The cloth and water form a cooling solution
    D. It does not read lower

    17.____

18. The color of the lubricating oil in a carbon dioxide refrigerating plant manufacturing dry ice is

    A. lemon yellow
    B. pale lemon
    C. lily or water white
    D. pale orange

19. In a packaged air conditioning unit, the refrigeration unit was overcharged.
    The result would be

    A. increased head pressure and suction pressure
    B. decreased head pressure
    C. low suction pressure
    D. low head and low suction pressure

20. The GREATEST operating capacity can be maintained by a MAXIMUM

    A. suction and discharge superheat
    B. discharge pressure
    C. suction pressure
    D. constant water flow to the system

21. An ammonia type compression system uses sea water as found in the New York Harbor for condensing service.
    In order to test for the presence of ammonia in this water, one should use _____ solution.

    A. Carrene
    B. sulphur
    C. Nessler's
    D. halide

22. A vertical single-acting compressor has pistons with suction valves. In this arrangement, only the top of the cylinder is water jacketed.
    The BEST reason for this is

    A. lower cost of the casting
    B. less water is used
    C. the lower part of the cylinder would be cooler than the jacket water
    D. only the discharge valves need cooling

23. In order to prevent rust or corrosion in a salt brine used to manufacture ice, an operator would add

    A. sodium dichromate
    B. aluminum sulphate
    C. Nessler's solution
    D. universal indicator solution

24. The brine in an icemaking plant will PROBABLY be between

    A. 0° and 11° C
    B. 0° and 11° F
    C. 25° and 29° C
    D. 14° and 22° F

25. In a reciprocating compressor, the pistons are of double trunk type. The ADVANTAGE of this is  25.____

    A. oil will not mix with refrigerant
    B. lighter piston
    C. more piston rings can be used
    D. shorter connecting rods

---

## KEY (CORRECT ANSWERS)

1. D
2. A
3. D
4. D
5. B

6. D
7. A
8. C
9. A
10. C

11. D
12. A
13. B
14. C
15. C

16. A
17. B
18. C
19. A
20. C

21. C
22. C
23. A
24. B
25. A

# EXAMINATION SECTION
# TEST 1

DIRECTIONS: Each question or incomplete statement is followed by several suggested answers or completions. Select the one that BEST answers the question or completes the statement. *PRINT THE LETTER OF THE CORRECT ANSWER IN THE SPACE AT THE RIGHT.*

1. Which of the following is the MOST likely action a supervisor should take to help establish an effective working relationship with his departmental superiors?
    A. Delay the implementation of new procedures received from superiors in order to evaluate their appropriateness.
    B. Skip the chain of command whenever he feels that it is to his advantage
    C. Keep supervisors informed of problems in his area and the steps taken to correct them
    D. Don't take up superiors' time by discussing anticipated problems but wait until the difficulties occur

    1._____

2. Of the following, the action a supervisor could take which would generally be MOST conducive to the establishment of an effective working relationship with employees includes
    A. maintaining impersonal relationships to prevent development of biased actions
    B. treating all employees equally without adjusting for individual differences
    C. continuous observation of employees on the job with insistence on constant improvement
    D. careful planning and scheduling of work for your employees

    2._____

3. Which of the following procedures is the LEAST likely to establish effective working relationships between employees and supervisors?
    A. Encouraging two-way communication with employees
    B. Periodic discussion with employees regarding their job performance
    C. Ignoring employees' gripes concerning job difficulties
    D. Avoiding personal prejudices in dealing with employees

    3._____

4. Criticism can be used as a tool to point out the weak areas of a subordinate's work performance.
   Of the following, the BEST action for a supervisor to take so that his criticism will be accepted is to
    A. focus his criticism on the act instead of on the person
    B. exaggerate the errors in order to motivate the employee to do better
    C. pass judgment quickly and privately without investigating the circumstances of the error
    D. generalize the criticism and not specifically point out the errors in performance

    4._____

5. In trying to improve the motivation of his subordinates, a supervisor can achieve the BEST results by taking action based upon the assumption that most employees
   A. have an inherent dislike of work
   B. wish to be closely directed
   C. are more interested in security than in assuming responsibility
   D. will exercise self-direction without coercion

6. When there are conflicts or tensions between top management and lower-level employees in any department, the supervisor should FIRST attempt to
   A. represent and enforce the management point of view
   B. act as the representative of the workers to get their ideas across to management
   C. serve as a two-way spokesman, trying to interpret each side to the other
   D. remain neutral, but keep informed of changes in the situation

7. A probationary period for new employees is usually provided in many agencies. The MAJOR purpose of such a period is usually to
   A. allow a determination of employee's suitability for the position
   B. obtain evidence as to employee's ability to perform in a higher position
   C. conform to requirements that ethnic hiring goals be met for all positions
   D. train the new employee in the duties of the position

8. An effective program of orientation for new employees usually includes all of the following EXCEPT
   A. having the supervisor introduce the new employee to his job, outlining his responsibilities and how to carry them out
   B. permitting the new worker to tour the facility or department so he can observe all parts of it in action
   C. scheduling meetings for new employees, at which the job requirements are explained to them and they are given personnel manuals
   D. testing the new worker on his skills and sending him to a centralized in-service workshop

9. In-service training is an important responsibility of many supervisors. The MAJOR reason for such training is to
   A. avoid future grievance procedures because employees might say they were not prepared to carry out their jobs
   B. maximize the effectiveness of the department by helping each employee perform at his full potential
   C. satisfy inspection teams from central headquarters of the department
   D. help prevent disagreements with members of the community

10. There are many forms of useful in-service training.
    Of the following, the training method which is NOT an appropriate technique for leadership development is to
    A. provide special workshops or clinics in activity skills
    B. conduct institutes to familiarize new workers with the program of the department and with their roles

C. schedule team meetings for problem-solving, including both supervisors and leaders
D. have the leader rate himself on an evaluation form periodically

11. Of the following techniques of evaluating work training programs, the one that is BEST is to
    A. pass out a carefully designed questionnaire to the trainees at the completion of the program
    B. test the knowledge that trainees have both at the beginning of training and at its completion
    C. interview the trainees at the completion of the program
    D. evaluate performance before and after training for both a control group and an experimental group

11._____

12. Assume that a new supervisor is having difficulty making his instructions to subordinates clearly understood.
    The one of the following which is the FIRST step he should take in dealing with this problem is to
    A. set up a training workshop in communication skills
    B. determine the extent and nature of the communications gap
    C. repeat both verbal and written instructions several times
    D. simplify his written and spoken vocabulary

12._____

13. A director has not properly carried out the orders of his assistant supervisor on several occasions to the point where he has been successively warned, reprimanded, and severely reprimanded.
    When the director once again does not carry out orders, the PROPER action for the assistant supervisor to take is to
    A. bring the director up on charges of failing to perform his duties properly
    B. have a serious discussion with the director, explaining the need for the orders and the necessity for carrying them out
    C. recommend that the director be transferred to another district
    D. severely reprimand the director again, making clear that no further deviation will be countenanced

13._____

14. A supervisor with several subordinates becomes aware that two of these subordinates are neither friendly nor congenial.
    In making assignments, it would be BEST for the supervisor to
    A. disregard the situation
    B. disregard the situation in making a choice of assignment but emphasize the need for teamwork
    C. investigate the situation to find out who is at fault and give that individual the less desirable assignments until such time as he corrects his attitude
    D. place the unfriendly subordinates in positions where they have as little contact with one another as possible

14._____

15. A DESIRABLE characteristic of a good supervisor is that he should  15.____
    A. identify himself with his subordinates rather than with higher management
    B. inform subordinates of forthcoming changes in policies and programs only when they directly affect the subordinates' activities
    C. make advancement of the subordinates contingent on personal loyalty to the supervisor
    D. make promises to subordinates only when sure of the ability to keep them

16. The supervisor who is MOST likely to be successful is the one who  16.____
    A. refrains from exercising the special privileges of his position
    B. maintains a formal attitude toward his subordinates
    C. maintains an informal attitude toward his subordinates
    D. represents the desires of his subordinate to his superiors

17. Application of sound principles of human relations by a supervisor may be expected to _____ the need for formal discipline.  17.____
    A. decrease
    B. have no effect on
    C. increase
    D. obviate

18. The MOST important generally approved way to maintain or develop high morale in one's subordinates is to  18.____
    A. give warnings and reprimands in a jocular way
    B. excuse from staff conferences those employees who are busy
    C. keep them informed of new developments and policies of higher management
    D. refrain from criticizing their faults directly

19. In training subordinates, an IMPORTANT principle for the supervisor to recognize is that  19.____
    A. a particular method of instruction will be of substantially equal value for all employees in a given title
    B. it is difficult to train people over 50 years of age because they have little capacity for learning
    C. persons undergoing the same course of training will learn at different rates of speed
    D. training can seldom achieve its purpose unless individual instruction is the chief method used

20. Over an extended period of time, a subordinate is MOST likely to become and remain most productive if the supervisor  20.____
    A. accords praise to the subordinate whenever his work is satisfactory, withholding criticism except in the case of very inferior work
    B. avoids both praise and criticism except for outstandingly good or bad work performed by the subordinate
    C. informs the subordinate of his shortcomings, as viewed by management, while according praise only when highly deserved
    D. keeps the subordinate informed of the degree of satisfaction with which his performance of the job is viewed by management.

## KEY (CORRECT ANSWERS)

1. C
2. D
3. C
4. A
5. D

6. C
7. A
8. D
9. B
10. D

11. D
12. B
13. A
14. D
15. D

16. D
17. A
18. C
19. C
20. D

# TEST 2

DIRECTIONS: Each question or incomplete statement is followed by several suggested answers or completions. Select the one that BEST answers the question or completes the statement. *PRINT THE LETTER OF THE CORRECT ANSWER IN THE SPACE AT THE RIGHT.*

1. A supervisor has just been told by a subordinate, Mr. Jones, that another employee, Mr. Smith, deliberately disobeyed an important rule of the department by taking home some confidential departmental material. Of the following courses of action, it would be MOST advisable for the supervisor FIRST to
   A. discuss the matter privately with both Mr. Jones and Mrs. Smith at the same time
   B. call a meeting of the entire staff and discuss the matter generally without mentioning any employee by name
   C. arrange to supervise Mr. Smith's activities more closely
   D. discuss the matter privately with Mr. Smith

   1.____

2. The one of the following actions which would be MOST efficient and economical for a supervisor to take to minimize the effect of periodical fluctuations in the workload of his unit is to
   A. increase his permanent staff until it is large enough to handle the work of the busy loads
   B. request the purchase of time- and labor-saving equipment to be used primarily during the busy loads
   C. lower, temporarily, the standards for quality of work performance during peak loads
   D. schedule for the slow periods work that is not essential to perform during the busy periods

   2.____

3. Discipline of employees is usually a supervisor's responsibility. There may be several useful forms of disciplinary action.
   Of the following, the form that is LEAST appropriate is the
   A. written reprimand or warning
   B. involuntary transfer to another work setting
   C. demotion or suspension
   D. assignment of added hours of work each week

   3.____

4. Of the following, the MOST effective means of dealing with employee disciplinary problems is to
   A. give personality tests to individuals to identify their psychological problems
   B. distribute and discuss a policy manual containing exact rules governing employee behavior
   C. establish a single, clear penalty to be imposed for all wrongdoing irrespective of degree
   D. have supervisors get to know employees well through social mingling

   4.____

5. A recently developed technique for appraising work performance is to have the supervisor record on a continual basis all significant incidents in each subordinate's behavior that indicate unsuccessful action and those that indicate poor behavior.
Of the following, a MAJOR disadvantage of this method of performance appraisal is that it
   A. often leads to overly close supervision
   B. results in competition among those subordinates being evaluated
   C. tends to result in superficial judgments
   D. lacks objectivity for evaluating performance

6. Assume that you are a supervisor and have observed the performance of an employee during a period of time. You have concluded that his performance needs improvement.
In order to improve his performance, it would, therefore, be BEST for you to
   A. note your findings in the employee's personnel folder so that his behavior is a matter of record
   B. report the findings to the personnel officer so he can take prompt action
   C. schedule a problem-solving conference with the employee
   D. recommend his transfer to simpler duties

7. When an employee's absences or latenesses seem to be nearing excessiveness, the supervisor should speak with him to find out what the problem is.
Of the following, if such a discussion produces no reasonable explanation, the discussion usually BEST serves to
   A. affirm clearly the supervisor's adherence to proper policy
   B. alert other employees that such behavior is unacceptable
   C. demonstrate that the supervisor truly represents higher management
   D. notify the employee that his behavior is being observed and evaluated

8. Assume that an employee willfully and recklessly violates an important agency regulation. The nature of the violation is of such magnitude that it demands immediate action, but the facts of the case are not entirely clear. Further, assume that the supervisor is free to make any of the following recommendations.
The MOST appropriate action for the supervisor to take is to recommend that the employee be
   A. discharged          B. suspended
   C. forced to resign    D. transferred

9. Although employees' titles may be identical, each position in that title may be considerably different.
Of the following, a supervisor should carefully assign each employee to a specific position based PRIMARILY on the employee's
   A. capability     B. experience     C. education     D. seniority

3 (#2)

10. The one of the following situations where it is MOST appropriate to transfer an employee to a similar assignment is one in which the employee
    A. lacks motivation and interest
    B. experiences a personality conflict with his supervisor
    C. is negligent in the performance of his duties
    D. lacks capacity or ability to perform assigned tasks

10.____

11. The one of the following which is LEAST likely to be affected by improvements in the morale of personnel is employee
    A. skill
    B. absenteeism
    C. turnover
    D. job satisfaction

11.____

12. The one of the following situations in which it is LEAST appropriate for a supervisor to delegate authority to subordinates is where the supervisor
    A. lacks confidence in his own abilities to perform certain work
    B. is overburdened and cannot handle all his responsibilities
    C. refers all disciplinary problems to his subordinate
    D. has to deal with an emergency or crisis

12.____

13. Assume that it has come to your attention that two of your subordinates have shouted at each other and have almost engaged in a fist fight. Luckily, they were separated by some of the other employees.
    Of the following, your BEST immediate course of action would generally be to
    A. reprimand the senior of the two subordinates since he should have known better
    B. hear the story from both employees and any witnesses and then take needed disciplinary action
    C. ignore the matter since nobody was physically hurt
    D. immediately suspend and fine both employees pending a departmental hearing

13.____

14. You have been delegating some of your authority to one of your subordinates because of his leadership potential.
    Which of the following actions is LEAST conducive to the growth and development of this individual for a supervisory position?
    A. Use praise only when it will be effective
    B. Give very detailed instructions and supervise the employee closely to be sure that the instructions ae followed precisely
    C. Let the subordinate proceed with his planned course of action even if mistakes, within a permissible range, are made
    D. Intervene on behalf of the subordinate whenever an assignment becomes difficult for him

14.____

15. A rumor has been spreading in your department concerning the possibility of layoffs due to decreased revenues.
    As a supervisor, you should GENERALLY
    A. deny the rumor, whether it is true or false, in order to keep morale from declining

15.____

B. inform the men to the best of your knowledge about this situation and keep them advised of any new information
C. tell the men to forget about the rumor and concentrate on increasing their productivity
D. ignore the rumor since it is not authorized information

16. Within an organization, every supervisor should know to whom he reports and who reports to him.
The one of the following which is achieved by use of such structured relationships is
    A. unity of command
    B. confidentiality
    C. esprit de corps
    D. promotion opportunities

17. Almost every afternoon, one of your employees comes back from his break ten minutes late without giving you any explanation.
Which of the following actions should you take FIRST in this situation?
    A. Assign the employee to a different type of work and observe whether his behavior changes
    B. Give the employee extra work to do so that he will have to return on time
    C. Ask the employee for an explanation for his lateness
    D. Tell the employee he is jeopardizing the break for everyone

18. When giving instructions to your employees in a group, which one of the following should you make certain to do?
    A. Speak in a casual, off-hand manner
    B. Assume that your employees fully understand the instructions
    C. Write out your instructions beforehand and read them to the employees
    D. Tell exactly who is to do what

19. A fist fight develops between two men under your supervision.
The MOST advisable course of action for you to take FIRST is to
    A. call the police
    B. have the other workers pull them apart
    C. order them to stop
    D. step between the two men

20. You have assigned some difficult and unusual work to one of your most experienced and competent subordinates.
If you notice that he is doing the work incorrectly, you should
    A. assign the work to another employee
    B. reprimand him in private
    C. show him immediately how the work should be done
    D. wait until the job is completed and then correct his errors

## KEY (CORRECT ANSWERS)

| | | | |
|---|---|---|---|
| 1. | D | 11. | A |
| 2. | D | 12. | C |
| 3. | D | 13. | B |
| 4. | B | 14. | B |
| 5. | A | 15. | B |
| 6. | C | 16. | A |
| 7. | D | 17. | C |
| 8. | B | 18. | D |
| 9. | A | 19. | C |
| 10. | B | 20. | C |

# THEORY OF HEAT

## CONTENTS

|  |  | Page |
|---|---|---|
| A. | INTRODUCTION | 1 |
| B. | MEASUREMENT OF HEAT | 1 |
| C. | KINDS OF HEAT | 2 |
| D. | PRESSURE | 4 |
| E. | VAPORIZATION | 6 |
| F. | PHYSICAL CONDITIONS OF VAPORS AND LIQUIDS | 7 |
| G. | EXPANSION AND CONTRACTION OF SUBSTANCE | 7 |
| H. | HEAT TRANSFER | 8 |
| I. | INSULATION | 9 |

# THEORY OF HEAT

## A. INTRODUCTION

**A1. General.**—As mentioned earlier, heat is a very relative term. Usually one thinks of it as a means of warming the body, or some object, to a desired temperature. Strange as it may seem, heat is ever present, even in a block of ice. In this chapter, heat is explained in terms of how it is used and transferred from substance to substance. Heat transfer is what all refrigeration systems are designed to accomplish. To understand the basic principles of refrigeration, it is most important that the student have a definite understanding of the relationship of heat, temperatures, and pressures.

**A2. Matter Defined.**—Matter is anything that has weight and occupies space. All substances are forms of matter in one of three stages: solid, liquid, or gaseous. An example of a substance in its three stages is water.

In its natural state water is a liquid. It has weight, volume, and takes the shape of the container which holds it. If it is heated in a closed container to its boiling point and more heat is added, it changes to steam or vapor which is its gaseous state. It has weight and occupies the volume or space of the container. When water is frozen, it becomes ice or is in its solid state. In this state, it has weight and volume, and it takes a definite shape.

Theoretically, all substances can be converted from one to another of the three states by the addition or withdrawal of heat. However, chemical compounds differ in the ease or difficulty with which they may be changed from one to another of the three physical states. Some, like water, can very readily be converted into each of the three states; others, like paper, oxidize, or burn, at high temperatures and cannot be converted into all three. Before paper burns, it changes to a gas, but never to a liquid. The science of refrigeration depends upon changes in physical state through heating or cooling.

**A3. Definition of Heat.**—Heat is a form of energy. It cannot be seen or shaped, nor can it be created or destroyed. It can only be transferred from substance to substance.

All substances are made up of tiny molecules. These molecules are in constant motion and moving against each other. As the temperature of these molecules increases, so does their activity, and as heat is taken away their activity and temperature decrease. If all heat is extracted from a substance (absolute zero temperature), the molecular motion will become dormant.

## B. MEASUREMENT OF HEAT

**B1. Intensity and Quantity.**—From experience we know that heat and temperature are related. If heat is added to a substance the temperature of the substance will rise, and if heat is taken away the temperature will decrease. There is a difference, however, in quantity and intensity. Heat is measured (1) by its intensity, and (2) by the quantity of it possessed by a substance. This is readily understood by comparing a spoonful of hot water with a pailful of warm water. The hot water in the spoon has a greater intensity of heat, but the warm water in the pail possesses a larger quantity of heat, though at a lower intensity.

**B2. Thermometer.**—Intensity of heat is measured by the ordinary thermometer with which everyone is familiar. The two methods of dividing and numbering the thermometer scales in common use are the Fahrenheit and the Centigrade. Another scale not so common but used by scientists is the Kelvin.

**B3. Fahrenheit Scale.**—The temperature scale most commonly used in refrigeration is the Fahrenheit scale represented by the designator °F. This scale is fixed to divide the

## THEORY OF HEAT

difference between melting ice and boiling water into 180 equal degrees. The melting ice is represented by a mark of 32° F, and boiling water at 212° F. Degrees above and below these are also equal divisions shown on the scale. When reaching the temperature where all molecular action in all substances ceases, a thermometer reading of -459.69° F would be indicated. This is called absolute zero. Scientists have been able, under controlled conditions, to measure temperatures within a few thousandths of absolute zero.

B4. **Centigrade Scale.**—The centigrade thermometer is scaled in degrees and indicated by °C. On this scale, ice melts at 0° C and water boils at 100° C. The 100 degrees between melting point and boiling point are equally divided on the scale. The absolute zero temperature on the centigrade scale is -273.16° C.

The centigrade scaled thermometer is used in most countries except the United States and Britain. It is used universally in scientific work.

B5. **Absolute or Kelvin Scale.**—The Kelvin scale is graduated in degrees starting at zero. On this scale, 0° K is equal to -273° C or -460° F, or absolute zero. The boiling point of water, 373° K, and the melting point of ice, 273° K, are equal to readings on the Fahrenheit and centigrade scales as shown in figure 1.

B6. **British Thermal Unit.**—The quantity of heat possessed by a substance is measured in terms of the British thermal unit, abbreviated Btu. A Btu is the quantity of heat required to raise the temperature of one pound of pure water one degree Fahrenheit at or near 39.10° F. This is the temperature at which water is at maximum density. For example, to raise the temperature of five pounds of water from 39° to 49° F, or from 160° to 170° F, requires 5 x 10 = 50 Btu. For all practical purposes, the Btu is considered constant between 32° and 212° F, though it does vary a slight amount.

### C. KINDS OF HEAT

C1. **General.**—To have an understanding of the terminology used in refrigeration and air conditioning, it is essential that the meaning of the terms discussed in this section be known. Some terms seem closely related, but the meaning and way they are applied is very important. The terms considered here apply to heat.

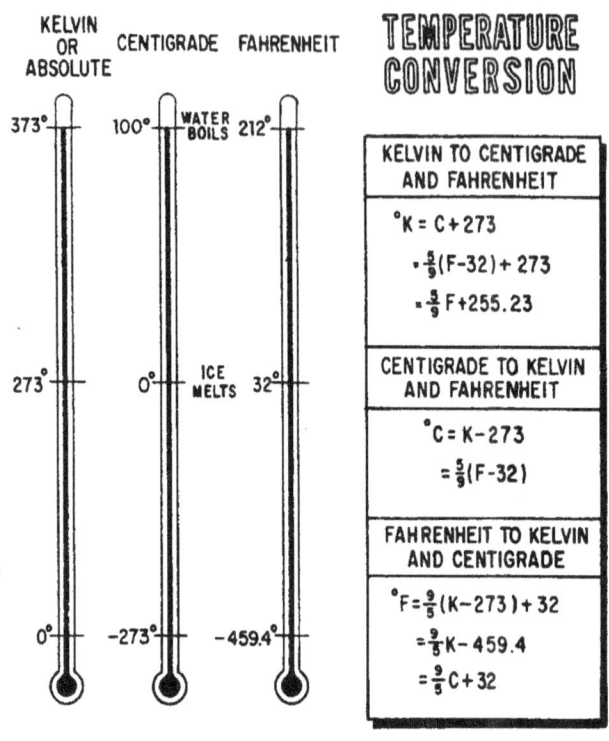

Figure 1.—Comparison of Fahrenheit, centigrade, and Kelvin temperature scales.

C2. **Specific Heat.**—Specific heat is the number of Btu that must be added to a unit weight of substance to raise its temperature 1 degree Fahrenheit. Since most substances held to a constant weight vary in volume, varying numbers of Btu are required to change the temperature 1 degree Fahrenheit per unit.

Technically, the specific heat of a substance is the ratio of the amount of heat required to change the temperature of a unit weight of that substance 1 degree to the amount of heat required to change the temperature of the same weight of water one degree. Since the specific heat of water is, by definition, equal to 1, the specific heat of other substances are expressed as decimals. Examples of the specific heat of some substances follow:

| Material | Specific Heat (Btu/Lb) |
|---|---|
| Wood | .327 |
| Ice | .504 |
| Iron | .129 |
| Copper | .095 |
| Glass | .187 |

Mercury .033
Alcohol .615
Liquid Ammonia at
40° F. 1.100

C3. **Thermal Capacity.**—Thermal capacity is closely related to specific heat. The specific heat of a substance is the number of Btu necessary to raise the temperature of one pound of the substance one degree Fahrenheit. The thermal capacity of a substance is the amount of heat required to raise the temperature of its whole mass one degree. Hence, thermal capacity equals the specific heat of a substance multiplied by its mass. Thermal capacity may be said to express the total capacity of a given quantity of a substance for absorbing and storing heat. Thermal capacity is stated, not as a ratio, but as a certain number of Btu.

C4. **Sensible Heat.**—Heat that is added to, or subtracted from, a substance that changes its temperature but not its physical state is called sensible heat. It is the heat that can be indicated on a thermometer. This is the heat which human senses also can react to, at least within certain ranges. For example, if a person puts his finger into a cup of water, his senses readily tell him whether it is cold, cool, tepid, hot, or very hot. Human senses are not sufficiently discriminating to give precise information about the extreme temperatures of ice and steam or other substances having temperatures beyond the range of human sensory mechanisms. Ice merely seems cold and steam seems hot whatever their temperatures. Sensible heat is applied to a solid (as ice), a liquid (as water), or a vapor/gas (as steam) as indicated on a thermometer. The term sensible heat does not apply to the process of conversion from one physical state to another.

C5. **Latent Heat.**—Heat absorbed, or given up, during the conversion of a substance from one physical state to another has another name. This is called latent heat. The term, latent heat, has two forms; latent heat of fusion and latent heat of vaporization.

Latent is taken from the Greek language meaning hidden. When latent heat is added to or subtracted from a substance, and the physical change takes place, there is no change in the sensible heat or temperature of the substance.

C6. **Latent Heat of Fusion.**—If heat is applied to a piece of ice at a temperature of 0° F, the temperature of the ice would gradually rise. This change in temperature, which can be indicated by placing a thermometer on the ice, is called sensible heat as stated previously. No change in state takes place, only a change in the temperature of the ice.

As more sensible heat is added, the temperature of the ice finally reaches 32° F. Now, as more heat is absorbed by the ice, the ice melts or changes state, but the temperature of the liquid is also 32° F. The heat added during the process of melting the ice at 32° to water at 32° F (at sea level barometric pressure) is the hidden or latent heat of fusion.

This process also works in the reverse order. When water is chilled to 32° F and more heat is taken away to form it into ice at 32° F, this heat is also latent heat of fusion.

Here is where one of the most important laws in physics is involved in refrigeration; heat can never be destroyed. It can only be transferred from one substance to another. So, the same amount of heat required to melt the ice into water must be removed from the water to convert it back to ice.

The latent heat of fusion for pure water at 32° F and at sea-level barometric pressure is 143.33 Btu per pound.

C7. **Latent Heat of Vaporization.**—As the last of the ice melts, the temperature of the water begins to rise. The temperature causing the rise is sensible heat. When the temperature of water reaches 212° F, the temperature stops rising and another change takes place. More heat is added and the water boils or changes to steam, but there is no change in temperature. This too is hidden heat. As the last of the water vaporizes and more heat is added, the temperature will again rise and again we are dealing with sensible heat.

The heat added to, or taken away, in the process of changing water to steam vapor, or from vapor/steam back to water, is called latent heat of vaporization. All substances that change from liquid to a vapor or gas go through this stage.

The value set for one pound of water at 212° F to be converted into steam, or steam converted to water, is 970.4 Btu. Other changes of state with variation of temperature, and the number of Btu required by such changes for a pound of water, are shown in figure 2.

## THEORY OF HEAT

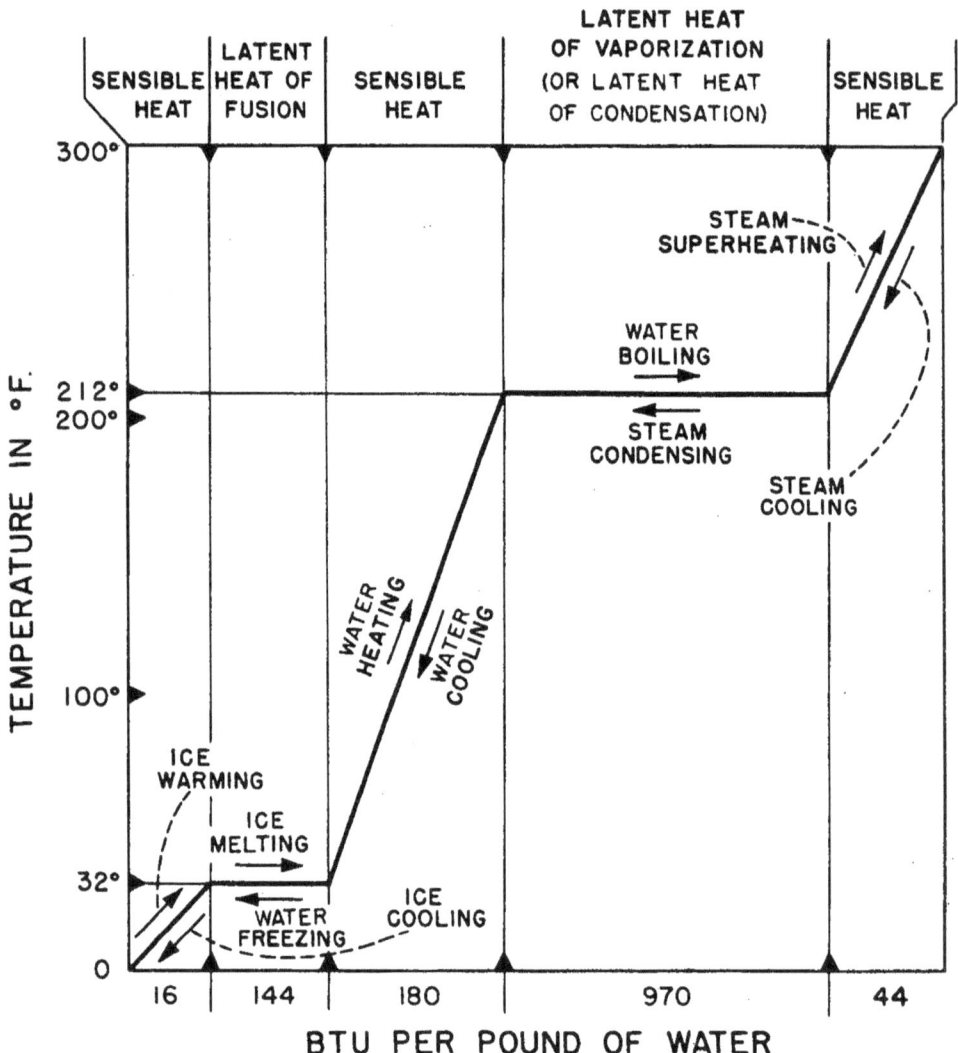

Figure 2.—Relationship between sensible heat and latent heat for water at atmospheric pressure.

C8. **Total Heat.**—The term <u>total heat</u> is used with two different meanings and care must be used in reading textbooks in order that the meaning intended is properly understood. These two usages are as follows:

Strictly speaking, the total heat of a substance is the total heat energy calculated from absolute zero in Btu. It is specific heat x mass x absolute temperature. Since there is no instrument, however, for measuring heat directly on the absolute scale, and since it would also require high numbers, other starting points are arbitrarily chosen. For the liquid water, the arbitrary starting point is 32° F.

In refrigeration and air conditioning, the total heat of a substance or of the air in a room is all the heat present, that is:

Total Heat = Sensible Heat + Latent Heat

In discussions, the term heat content is sometimes used. This term has the same meaning as total heat.

### D. PRESSURE

D1. **Atmospheric Pressure.**—At the beginning of this chapter, we defined matter as anything which occupies space and has weight. As air is matter, it too has weight. The weight of this air is called atmospheric pressure. The valued scale for a column of air 1 inch square in cross-sectional area at the base and reaching from sea level to the upper limit of the earth's atmosphere at 32° F and at sea level is 14.696 pounds. This will vary due to condition changes in the air above the earth. For all practical purposes, the value is considered to be 14.7 pounds per square inch (psi) at sea level.

D2. **Mercury Barometer.**—To measure atmospheric pressure, scientists have developed a simple instrument called a mercury barometer. It is constructed with a glass tube that is a little over thirty inches long and sealed at one end. The tube is then completely filled with mercury. By placing a finger over the open end and inverting into an open dish of mercury, the mercury column in the tube will fall, leaving a vacuum in the space above the mercury. The air pressure exerted on the surface of the mercury in the dish will maintain a column of mercury in the tube equal to the pressure on the surface. At sea level pressure of 14.7 psi, the height of the column of mercury in the tube will be 29.921 inches. As atmospheric pressure is increased or decreased, the height of the mercury column will vary in relation to the pressure.

D3. **Aneroid Barometer.**—Another device used to measure atmospheric pressure is the aneroid barometer. This type is more compact and easier to handle than the mercury barometer, but not as accurate.

The aneroid barometer consists of an airtight metal box, with a partial vacuum inside, and a flexible side that can move slightly under varying pressures. The motion of the flexible side is transmitted through gears and levers to a pointer that is calibrated to a scale on the dial. This scale is graduated in inches and corresponds to the inches of mercury in the mercury barometer.

A good aneroid barometer will show a slight increase in pressure when lowered from a table to the floor.

D4. **Conversion of Barometer Readings.**— Since the aneroid and mercury barometers indicate the atmospheric pressure in inches, a conversion factor must be used to convert this pressure to pounds per square inch. At an air temperature of 32° F and at mean sea level, the mercury column stands at 29.921 inches and corresponds to a pressure of 14.696 psi. By dividing 14.696 by 29.921, the result will give the conversion factor of 0.491. To convert the reading on the barometer, multiply the reading by the conversion factor.

D5. **Variation of Pressure and Boiling Point with Altitude.**—The pressures and boiling points of substances will vary with altitudes. If an uncovered container filled with fresh water at mean sea level is heated until the water boils, a thermometer inserted in the water shows that its temperature is 212° F, and a barometer shows that the atmospheric pressure is approximately 14.7 psi. However, if the pot of boiling water is on a hilltop 1000 feet above sea level, the thermometer shows that the water boils at 210° F when the barometer reads approximately 14.14 psi. Similar variations in boiling point and barometric pressure are observed at different altitudes, as indicated in the following table:

| Feet above sea level | Pressure (psi) | Boiling point of Water (°F) |
|---|---|---|
| Sea level | 14.70 | 212 |
| 2000 | 13.57 | 208 |
| 4000 | 12.49 | 204 |
| 6000 | 11.54 | 200 |
| 8000 | 10.62 | 196 |

D6. **Pressure-Temperature Relationship for Change of State.**—It is not variations of pressure and temperatures at different altitudes to which special attention is directed, but the relationship between the temperature of vaporization and the corresponding pressure. It is not necessary, however, to go to different heights to obtain different pressures; different pressures may be obtained by mechanical means at any location.

For example, a boiling liquid and its vapor may be contained in an airtight metal cylinder with a piston. By moving the piston in or out, the pressure within may be increased or decreased. If the piston is pushed in, thus increasing the pressure inside, a thermometer shows that the change of state from liquid to vapor requires a temperature higher than 212° F. If the piston is pulled out, thus decreasing the pressure within, the thermometer shows that the change of state from liquid to vapor takes

## THEORY OF HEAT

place at a temperature lower than 212° F. Many types of such mechanical arrangements are in common use.

This relationship of vaporization temperature and pressure, which varies for different substances, follows an exact law, and may be tabulated accurately for each substance.

D7. **Pressure Gage.**—Pressures within an airtight system of pipes, tanks, and cylinders are usually measured by a Bourdon-tube pressure gage. In this gage there is a small tube, flattened (not round) in cross-section, and curved to about three-quarters of a circle. One end of this curved tube is firmly fixed to the mounting, or case; the other end is free and slightly movable. A delicate lever system which turns a pointer on a circular scale is attached to the free end. The fixed end of this tube is joined by connections to the vapor system, and made part of that system. Increases in vapor pressure tend to straighten the curved tube, thus rotating the pointer. The scale is marked to indicate the pressure values in units of pounds per square inch.

The scale on the Bourdon-tube pressure gage is marked with zero to correspond to standard atmospheric pressure. Consequently, zero gage pressure equals 14.7 pounds per square inch. When the pressure of the vapor inside the curved tube is 14.7 psi, it is equal to the atmospheric pressure outside the tube, and there is no tendency for the curved tube to straighten. Hence, this pressure is taken as the zero point on the gage.

'D8. **Gage Pressure.**—The pressure indicated by a Bourdon-tube pressure gage is in reality the difference between the vapor pressure inside and the air pressure outside the curved tube. Readings from such a gage are always designated gage pressure.

Gage pressure is expressed in pounds per square inch. For convenience, this term is indicated by its abbreviated form psi. Often, where the meaning is unmistakable, the word pounds alone is used; for example, 20 pounds' pressure means 20 pounds per square inch pressure.

D9. **Absolute Pressure.**—The term absolute pressure is used to designate the true total pressure inside the enclosed vapor system. Suppose the pressure gage stands at 6 pounds. Then, since zero gage pressure means 14.7 pounds inside (to balance 14.7 pounds air pressure outside the tube), the total, or absolute pressure of the vapor is 14.7 pounds plus 6 pounds, or 20.7 pounds. If an accurate knowledge of the pressure is required, the atmospheric pressure, converted from a barometer reading, is used instead of the 14.7-pound standard.

D10. **Vacuum or Negative Gage Pressure.**—As stated, the standard atmospheric pressure of 14.7 psi is taken as the zero point on the gage. A gage dealing only with increases in pressure has a single scale marked from 0 to 300 pounds, or some other upper limit, and is read in psi gage pressure.

But, pressures may decrease below atmospheric pressure as well as increase. Pressures below 14.7 psi are known as partial vacuums. This term is merely for convenience in referring to pressures below ordinary atmospheric pressure, since such a pressure is far from approaching a vacuum.

A gage that registers pressures lower than standard atmospheric pressure is called a vacuum gage. Such gages are graduated to read in inches of vacuum. Approximately 30 inches of vacuum equal zero pounds absolute pressure.

D11. **Compound Gage.**—A compound gage is sometimes called a compound pressure and vacuum gage. It has an extended range covering pressures both below and above atmospheric pressure. The scale is graduated to the left and right of zero (atmospheric pressure). Above atmospheric pressure readings are in psi, and below atmospheric pressures are readings of inches of vacuum.

Gages used on the suction side of most refrigeration units are of the compound type.

### E. VAPORIZATION

E1. **Kinds of Vaporization.**—Ebullition, evaporation, and sublimation are the three kinds of vaporization, or methods of converting from one physical state to another.

E2. **Ebullition.**—Ebullition is the technical term for ordinary boiling. It is a rapid and visible process. By looking into an uncovered container of boiling water, one can see that ebullition, or boiling, is taking place. Starting from the bottom and sides, large and small bubbles rise to the surface and escape from the liquid.

E3. Evaporation.—Evaporation is a slow and invisible process which takes place only from the surface of a liquid. Under ordinary conditions, evaporation cannot be seen. Any liquid in an uncovered container will gradually evaporate, its level slowly falling until all liquid is gone. Water continually evaporates from the surface of all open bodies such as rivers, lakes, ponds, and oceans. Wet clothing, hung on a line to dry, does so, by this process.

Since evaporation is a form of vaporization, it results in the removal of latent heat. Therefore, it is a cooling process, though a slow one. When a person goes in swimming on a cool day with a wind blowing, it is the evaporation process that makes him feel uncomfortable, rather than the temperature itself. The human body gets rid of excess heat and moisture naturally and continually by evaporation.

Some liquids evaporate much faster than others. For example, alcohol will evaporate much faster than water.

E4. Sublimation.—The third method of converting from one physical state to another is called sublimation. It consists of converting from a solid directly to the vapor state without passing through the intermediate or liquid state. Ice and snow, even when much below the freezing point, slowly disappear without melting. Washed clothes, hung out-of-doors in temperatures below 32° F, first freeze stiff, and then dry soft. Both these phenomena are caused by sublimation.

Sublimation has little application to refrigeration engineering. It has, however, considerable use in the small scale cooling of bottled goods, ice cream, and other food stuffs by the use of solid carbon dioxide, or dry ice, which sublimes to a vapor under atmospheric pressure.

E5. Vapor and Gas.—The terms vapor and gas both refer to matter in the physical state that is neither solid or liquid. There is, however, a definite distinction between the two.

Vapor condenses very readily to a liquid state under small changes of temperature or pressure, or both, and constantly does so under ordinary conditions of nature. It may be said to be very close to the liquid state, although it is a vapor.

Gas, on the other hand, exists under ordinary conditions in a gaseous state. To change it to a liquid state, special laboratory apparatus capable of producing extreme changes of pressure is required. A gas may be said to be far removed from the liquid state and cannot change under ordinary natural conditions.

In refrigeration, the word gas is frequently used instead of the more correct term vapor.

## F. PHYSICIAL CONDITIONS OF VAPORS AND LIQUIDS

F1. State and Condition.—The term state is used to refer to the three forms of matter: solid, liquid, and gas or vapor. However, a substance in any one of the three states may be found in different conditions. Hence, the term condition is also used. A vapor ordinarily exists in either of two conditions, as a saturated vapor or as superheated vapor.

F2. Saturated Vapor.—The saturated vapor is a vapor at the temperature corresponding to its boiling point at a given pressure. Saturated vapors are classed as either wet or dry. If they contain liquid particles of their substance, they are termed wet. If no particles are present, they are termed dry.

Saturated vapors are usually in the wet state due to the boiling action of the substance. The bubbles, as they break away from the surface as a vapor, will carry tiny droplets of the liquid suspended in the vapor.

F3. Superheated Vapor.—If a vapor is not in contact with a boiling liquid, either because the liquid has been converted into vapor or because the vapor has been separated from the boiling liquid, further application of heat produces a rise in temperature of the vapor under the same given pressure. Such a vapor is called superheated vapor.

F4. Saturation Temperature.—If a liquid is heated, it finally boils at a temperature that is the result of the pressure present. Such a temperature is called the saturation temperature corresponding to the given pressure. This term is frequently used in air conditioning and means the boiling point, or the condensation point, at the given pressure.

A liquid that is at the saturation temperature corresponding to a given pressure, and is under that pressure, is called a saturated liquid.

## G. EXPANSION AND CONTRACTION OF SUBSTANCE

G.1. General.—In general, all substances, whether solid, liquid, or gas, decrease in volume

## THEORY OF HEAT

when cooled and increase in volume when heated. In gases and vapors, the amount of change is large; in liquids and solids it is small. In all cases, great forces are produced and it is necessary in all engineering construction to allow for the operation of these forces. Different substances vary in the amount of change in volume they undergo for the same differences in temperature.

G2. **Expansion and Contraction of Water.**—Water contracts as it is cooled until the temperature 39.2°F is reached. At this point the change in volume reverses and if the water is cooled further, the volume increases. When water freezes into ice, an enormous force is brought into play. This force is sufficient to split large rocks, burst iron pipes and even steel tanks, unless provisions are allowed for the expansion.

G3. **Expansion and Contraction at the Change of State.**—At their melting point, substances follow no general rule regarding expansion and contraction. Some metals like iron, bismuth, and antimony, contract on melting and expand on solidifying; but most others like gold, silver, and copper, expand on melting and contract on solidifying. All liquids, however, expand greatly when changing into a vapor unless constrained mechanically, as in a closed container. An example of this expansion is the large clouds of steam continually rising from a container of boiling water.

G4. **Specific Volume.**—The specific volume of a substance is a number that indicates the number of cubic feet occupied by one pound of the substance at a given temperature and pressure. Specific volume varies greatly for different substances and for the same substances at different temperatures and pressures.

The specific volume for boiling water at atmospheric pressure is 0.0167 cubic feet per pound, and of steam at the same pressure it is 26.79 cubic feet per pound. Thus, water in changing its state from liquid to vapor at ordinary atmospheric pressure increases in volume 1604 times.

### H. HEAT TRANSFER

H1. **How Heat is Transferred.**—As explained earlier in this chapter, heat can neither be created nor destroyed, but only transferred from one substance to another. This transfer is accomplished through one of three ways: radiation, convection, and conduction.

H2. **Radiation.**—In radiation, heat is transmitted through empty space (a vacuum), as from the sun to the earth's atmosphere. Heat, light, electricity, radio, and x-rays are all known to be energy in the form of transverse vibrations. Physically, they differ only in their wave lengths, but their physical effects are quite different, as is evident by comparing heat with radio waves. In radiation, nothing but energy really travels.

Radiation does not heat the air through which it passes, it heats only the objects on which it falls. Not only the sun, but other objects such as flames, stoves, electric light bulbs, machines, and the earth itself, radiate heat. Even our bodies radiate heat.

H3. **Convection.**—Convection is the transfer of heat by the movement of a substance (gas or liquid) through a space. Examples of this include a current of warm air in a room, a current of warm water such as the Gulf Stream, and warm air rising from a hot water or steam radiator.

H4. **Conduction.**—The transfer of heat from one molecule to another, either of the same substance or of different substances, by direct contact is called conduction. A molecule of a substance is the smallest particle of a substance that retains the special qualities of that substance. Any further subdivision of a molecule separates it into the atoms of which it is composed.

Physical contact is necessary for conduction of heat, and the conduction takes place from the region of the higher temperature to the lower temperature. For example, if a person holds a metal bar of iron in one hand and places the other end of the bar in a fire, the heat passes from the fire to the bar, then along the bar to the hand. Here physical contact is made in each instance; fire to bar, bar to hand.

H5. **Thermal Conductance.**—Suppose that two bars are held, one of iron and one of copper, of exactly the same size and at the same temperature. If one end of each bar is placed in a fire at the same time, heat will reach the hand holding the copper bar more quickly than through the iron bar. This is because some substances conduct heat more readily than others.

This characteristic of a substance is called its thermal or heat conductance. The low and high thermal conductance of substances is of great importance in refrigeration and air conditioning. Some substances are used for transfer of heat while others are used to prevent heat transfer.

## I. INSULATION

11. **Need for Insulation.**—It is comparatively easy to heat or cool articles or enclosed spaces. It is not easy, however, to keep them at a constant temperature because heat constantly tends to flow to the lower temperature areas.

When it is desired to keep a space within a certain temperature range, it is necessary to prevent the transfer of heat to or from the space. Fortunately this can be done, fairly successfully, by the use of a substance with low thermal conductance.

12. **Insulators.**—Poor conductors are good insulators. Poor conductors include such substances as cork, wood, sawdust, paper, brick, rubber, fur, feathers, felt, plastics, cotton, and dead air space. Most solids that are poor conductors are also porous in nature, and the pores or air cells are small in size. Much of the insulating quality results from these tiny pockets.

The "K" conductivity factor for an insulating material is the amount of Btu per square foot, per hour, per °F, that can penetrate the insulation for a thickness of one inch. Some of the more commonly used insulating materials and "K" conductivity factors follow:

| Material | "K" Factor |
|---|---|
| Cork with pitch | 0.428 |
| Sawdust, pine | 0.57 |
| Wool, pure | 0.26 |
| Glass | 5.0 |
| Air (dead) | 0.175 |

13. **Low Temperature Insulation.**—The requirements for low-temperature insulation are somewhat different from those for high-temperature insulation. Any water vapor present in the air tends to condense into liquid droplets or film on a cold surface. This is commonly called sweating. This condensed water penetrates a porous material and fills the air cells, lessening its insulating ability. It may freeze there and ice is a very poor insulator of heat. Insulating materials for use with refrigeration systems are manufactured to resist the penetration of moisture, and to be durable under conditions of high humidity.

Low-temperature pipe lines must be thoroughly insulated to prevent heat from entering the refrigerant contained therein. The usual insulation is a cork composition molded into sections that fit snugly around the pipes and fittings. Other materials, such as rock wool and mineral wool, are also used in the same way.

Before applying the covering, all pipes should be carefully cleaned, all rust removed, and dried. If possible, the hangers and braces should be attached around the outside of the insulation to prevent the transfer of heat by conduction and to prevent moisture from entering the insulation.

When molded sections are installed on pipe lines, they should be staggered and all joints should be placed so as to come together at the top and bottom of the pipe. After all seams are sealed, the covering should be painted with an asphalt paint, to make it waterproof.

Always repair ruptured insulation as soon as possible to prevent the entry of moisture. Make sure the pipe is dry and all seams are sealed when making repairs.

# THE REFRIGERATION CYCLE

Mechanical refrigeration is used to remove heat from a colder medium and reject it to a warmer medium by using the latent heat properties of the refrigerant. Simply stated, in order to accomplish this transfer of heat energy, the refrigeration system must provide a refrigerant temperature below the temperature of the medium to be cooled and raise the temperature of the refrigerant to a level above the temperature of the medium that is used for rejection. Although the entire chiller package is more complex, the basic components required for mechanical refrigeration are the compressor, evaporator, condenser and thermostatic expansion valve. A complete typical chiller layout follows this section.

The P-H chart is an important tool in understanding the property changes that take place during each phase of the cycle and provides a graphical means of study. Horizontal lines on the P-H Chart are lines of constant pressure and vertical lines are lines of constant enthalpy

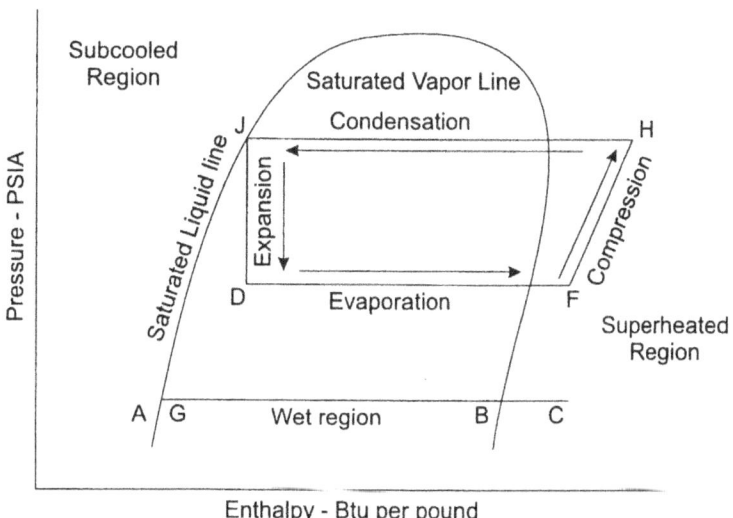

or heat energy. The line labeled "Saturated liquid line" and "Saturated Vaopr Line" are plots of the pressure-vs-enthalpy for the saturated state of a given refrigerant. The chart is divided into three regions. The area to the left is the subcooled region, to the right is the superheated region and in the middle is the wet region or mixture state. The constant temperature lines are horizontal in the mixture region indicating that phase change occurs at constant pressure. Likewise, expansion of the gas takes place at constant enthalpy.

Following the chart, if refrigerant liquid at point A absorbs heat at constant pressure, it will begin to boil. Evaporation takes place with no change in temperature. As heat is added, the enthalpy increases and it enters a mixture state of vapor and liquid. At point B, the mixture becomes a saturated vapor. Any additional heat applied at constant pressure causes the refrigerant to enter the superheat region indicated by point C.

In evaporation, the refrigerant enters the evaporator as a mixture of vapor and liquid at point D of the chart. It enters the evaporator by being metered through a thermostatic expansion valve, TXV, which lowers it's pressure and therefore its temperature. Because the refrigerant is at a temperature below the process fluid, it absorbs heat from the process fluid, and boils, and changed phase from a liquid to a gas. In order for the refrigerant to change state, it must take in heat energy. During this transfer of heat energy, only latent heat is absorbed resulting in the refrigerant remaining at a constant temperature. In theory, it leaves the evaporator as a vapor at point E, however, in application, additional heat, called "superheat" is added to prevent liquid condensation in the lines that can damage the compressor.

After absorbing the latent heat during evaporation and superheating, the refrigerant gas is compressed from a low pressure gas to a high pressure gas. During the compression process, the refrigerant gas absorbs additional heat known as the Heat of Compression, which is merely the friction of molecules being rapidly forced into a confined space. The additional heat energy caused by compression is represented by the line between points F and H. Note that point H is to the right of point F, indicating the additional enthalpy resulting from the Heat of Compression.

The now hot, high pressure gas is passed through a condenser to remove the heat of compression plus the latent heat of evaporation, collectively known as the "Total Heat of Rejection", or THR. This heat is typically rejected to a water source in the case of a water cooled chiller package, or to ambient air in an air cooled condenser package. From the P-H chart, it can be seen that condensation takes place at constant pressure. The heat transfer is represented by the difference in enthalpy between points H and J. At point J the refrigerant is totally condensed into a liquid and remains at constant pressure.

Superheat is the heat added to the vapor beyond what is required to vaporize all of the liquid. Superheat therefore is not latent, but sensible heat and is measured in degrees. From the chart below, it can be seen that superheat from the evaporation phase has a corresponding increase in the total heat of rejection at the condenser and results in the compressor operating at higher temperature. While some amount of superheat is required to protect the refrigeration system and prevent liquid entering the compressor, too much superheat can contribute to oil breakdown and increased system downtime.

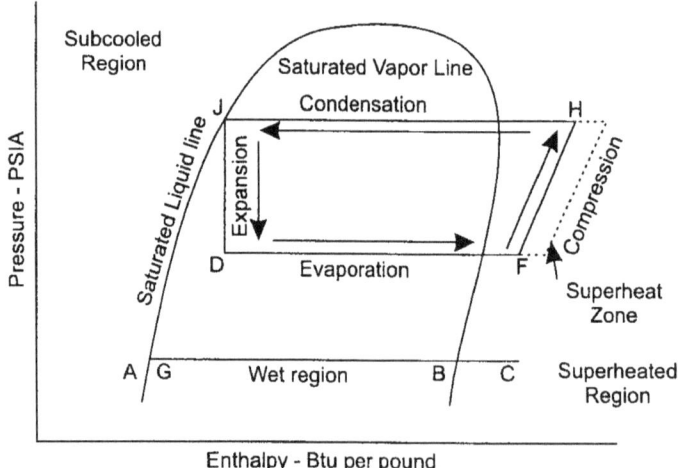

Subcooling is the process of cooling condensed gas beyond what is required for the condensation process. Subcooling is sensible heat and is measured in degrees. Subcooling can have a dramatic effect in the capacity of a refrigeration system by increasing the capacity of the refrigerant to absorb heat during the evaporation phase for the same compressor Kw input.

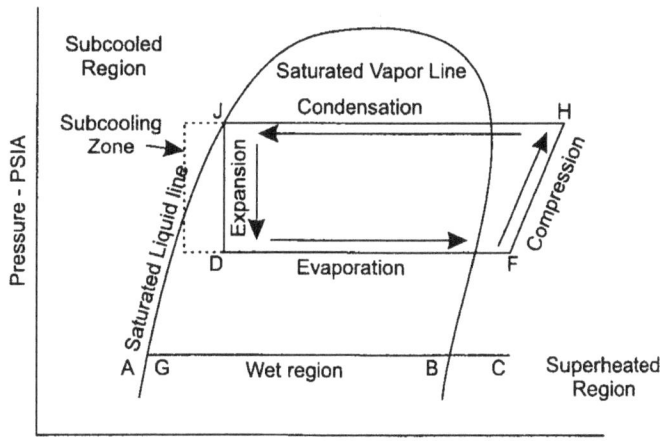

Subcooling assures that no gas is left at the end of the condensing phase, thus assuring maximum capacity at the TXV. Subcooling is best accomplished in a separate subcooler or a special subcooling section of a condenser because tube surface must be submerged in liquid refrigerant for subcooling to occur. Simply adding additional surface to a condenser is therefore not as effective. API manufactures a line of subcooling heat exchangers as well as special condensers with a condensing section and a subcooling section divided by a plate. Refrigerant is forced across the condensing section and then downward through the submerged tube section. It is important to pipe the condenser with the coldest water inlet countercurrent to the subcooling section.

As the high pressure cooled liquid from the condenser is reduced in pressure at the TXV, its corresponding temperature is reduced and the cycle is complete. It can be seen from the P-H chart that the heat load on the condenser is greater than that of the evaporator, or process load. This process load is traditionally expressed in "tons of refrigeration" and is equal to 12,000 Btu's per hour. Process heat loads can be calculated by several methods including:

**For clean water:  Btuh = GPM x 500 x temperature change**

**For other fluids:  Btuh = Lbs per hour x Specific Heat x temperature change**

The condenser load, or THR is this 12,000 Btuh plus the heat of compression which is derived based on the compressor type.

**For semi-hermetic compressors:**    Full load kW x 3,413 Btuh per kW

**For open drive compressors:**    Brake HP x 2,544 Btuh per HP

**Note: Tower cells are rated at 15,000 Btuh per ton**

*Example:*

Cool 300 GPM of water from 60°F to 50°F with a 100 HP open drive R-22 chiller. The process heat load is:

**300 GPM x 500 x 10° = 1,500,000 Btuh or 125 tons of refrigeration**

The condenser load is:

**(100 HP x 2,544 Btuh/HP) + 1,500,000 = 1,754,000 Btuh or 116.9 tower cell tons**

Special Note:

The actual enthalpy capacity for R-22 operating at 105°F condensing temperature and 40°F saturated suction temperature is 14,400 Btu/Ton. Correction factors must be applied for other operating conditions and refrigerants. Tower cell manufacturers have established a widely used standard of 15,000 Btu per ton. This value is not to be confused with tons of refrigeration used for chiller process load calculations which is 12,000 Btu/ton.

## Condenser Considerations

Water cooled condensers are typically specified when a supply of cooling water from a tower, lake, river or other source is readily available. Due to the cost of city water, water treatment, pumping costs and maintenence of a water delivery system, air cooled condensing is preferred in applications where service water is not required for other plant operations or where existing heat rejection capacity is insufficient.

Other reasons for selecting water cooled equipment are:

1. The refrigeration system consumes less electrical energy because the compression ratio is less. An air cooled condenser requires some potential temperature difference in order to reject heat, so the refrigeration system must operate at a higher head pressure and temperature to produce this temperature difference. Air cooled condensers normally requires between 125°F to 130°F condensing temperature to reject heat to a 100° ambient, while a water cooled condenser can operate at 105°F condensing temperature and reject its heat to a 95°F water stream. Because air is a poor conductor of heat, water cooled condensers can operate with a much lower approach temperature.

2. Water cooled condensers are much more compact and require no remote outdoor mounting and piping, rooftop structural preparation or outdoor NEMA-4 electrical service. Where equipment room floor space is at a premium, self contained air cooled chillers, or remote split systems are preferred.

3. Heat recovery is easier to obtain and control when using a water cooled condenser because the heat energy is more easily transported. Heated water from the refrigeration cycle can be diverted to heat other processes and even provide space heating during winter months.

# GLOSSARY OF ENGINEERING TERMS

## TABLE OF CONTENTS

| | Page |
|---|---|
| Automatic Bus Transfer ... Boiler Tube Cleaner | 1 |
| Boiler Water ... Distillate | 2 |
| Distilling Plants ... Forging | 3 |
| Fresh Water System ... Log Book | 4 |
| Log, Engineering ... Parts Per Million | 5 |
| Preheating ... Static | 6 |
| Steam Lance ... Wireways | 7 |
| Work Request ... Zinc | 8 |

# GLOSSARY OF ENGINEERING TERMS

ABT (AUTOMATIC BUS TRANSFER): An automatic electrical device that supplies power to vital equipment. This device will shift from the normal power supply to an alternate power supply when the normal supply is interrupted.

ACETYLENE: A gas that is chemically produced from calcium carbide and water, used for welding and cutting.

ADAPTER: A coupling or similar device that permits fittings with different-sized openings (apertures) to be joined together.

AIR EJECTOR: A type of jet pump, used to remove air and other gases from the condensers.

AIR CHAMBER: A chamber, usually bulb-shaped, on the suction and discharge sides of a pump. Air in the chamber acts as a cushion and prevents sudden shocks to the pump.

AIR REGISTER: A device in the casing of a boiler, used for regulating the amount of air for combustion and to provide a circular motion to the air.

AISE: Association of Iron and Steel Engineers.

ALLOY: A mixture composed of two or more metals.

ALTERNATING CURRENT (A-C): Current that is constantly changing in value and direction at regular recurring intervals.

AMBIENT TEMPERATURE: The temperature of the surrounding area.

AMMETER: An instrument for measuring the rate of flow of electrical current in amperes.

ANNEALING: The softening of metal by heating and slow cooling.

ANNUNCIATOR: See ENGINE ORDER TELEGRAPH.

ARGON: An inert gas, slightly heavier than air, used in inert-gas shielded metal arc welding.

ARMORED CABLE: An electric cable that is protected on the outside by a metal covering.

ASTM: American Society for Testing Metals.

AUTOMATIC COMBUSTION CONTROL SYSTEM (ACC): A system that provides a means of automatically controlling the fuel and air mixture in a boiler.

BACK PRESSURE: The pressure exerted on the exhaust side of a pump or engine.

BDC (BOTTOM DEAD CENTER): The position of a reciprocating piston at its lowest point of travel.

BALLASTING: The process of filling empty tanks with salt water, to protect the ship from underwater damage and increase its stability. See DEBALLASTING.

BLUEPRINTS: Reproduced copies of drawings (usually having white lines on a blue background.

BOILER: A strong' metal tank or vessel composed of tubes, drums, and headers, in which water is heated by the gases of combustion to form steam.

BOILER CENTRAL CONTROL STATION: A centrally located station for directing the control of all boilers in the fireroom.

BOILER DESIGN PRESSURE: Pressure specified by the manufacturer, usually about 103% of normal steam drum operating pressure.

BOILER INTERNAL FITTINGS: All parts inside the boiler which control the flow of steam and water.

BOILER OPERATING PRESSURE: The pressure required to be maintained in a boiler while in service.

BOILER OPERATING STATION: A location from which boilers are operated.

BOILER RECORD SHEET: A NavShips form maintained for each boiler, which serves as a monthly summary of operation.

BOILER REFRACTORIES: Materials used in the boiler furnace to protect the boiler from heat of combustion.

BOILER ROOM: A compartment containing boilers but not containing a station for operating or firing the boilers. Refers specifically to bulkhead enclosed boiler installations.

BOILER TUBE CLEANER: A CYLINDRICAL brush that is used to clean the insides of boiler tubes.

**BOILER WATER:** Refers to the water actually contained in the boiler.

**BRAZING:** A method of joining two metals at high temperature with a molten alloy.

**BRINE:** A highly concentrated solution of salt in water, normally associated with the overboard discharge of distilling plants.

**BRITTLENESS:** That property of a material which causes it to fracture prior to any noticeable signs of deformation.

**BURNERMAN:** Man in fireroom who tends the burners in the boilers.

**BUSHING:** A renewable lining for a hole through which a moving part passes.

**BYPASS:** To divert the flow of gas or liquid. Also, the line that diverts the flow.

**CALIBRATION:** The comparison of any measuring instrument with a set standard.

**CANTILEVER:** A projecting arm or beam supported only at one end.

**CAPILLARY TUBE:** A slender thin-walled small-bored tube used with remote-reading indicators.

**CARBON DIOXIDE:** A colorless, orderless gas used as a fire extinguishing agent and for inflating liferafts and lifejackets.

**CARBON PACKING:** Pressed segments of graphite used to prevent steam leakage around shafts.

**CASUALTY POWER SYSTEM:** A means of using portable cables to transmit power to vital equipment in an emergency.

**CHECK VALVE:** A valve that permits a flow of liquid in one direction only.

**CHILL SHOCKING:** A method of removing scale from the tubes of a distilling plant, utilizing steam and cold water.

**CHLORINE:** A heavy gas, greenish-yellow in color used for water purification, sewage disposal, and in the preparation of bleaching solutions. Poisonous in concentrated form.

**CIRCUIT BREAKER:** An electrical device that provides circuit overload protection.

**CLUTCH:** A form of coupling which is designed to connect or disconnect a driving or driven member.

**COMPARTMENT CHECKOFF LIST:** A list of all damage control fittings, their location, and status for different ship conditions.

**CONDENSER:** A heat transfer device in which steam or vapor is condensed to water.

**CONDUCTION:** A method of heat transfer from one body to another when the two bodies are in physical contact.

**CONSTANT PRESSURE GOVERNOR:** A device that maintains a constant pump discharge pressure under varying loads.

**CONTROLLER:** A device used to stop, start, and protect motors from overloads, while they are running.

**CORROSION:** The process of being eaten away gradually by chemical action, such as rusting.

**COUNTERSINK:** A cone-shaped tool used to enlarge and bevel one end of a drilled hole.

**CROSS-CONNECTED PLANT:** A method of operating two or more plants as one unit, having a common steam supply.

**CURTIS STAGE:** A velocity-compounded impulse turbine stage having one pressure drop in the nozzles and two velocity drops in the blading.

**DEAERATING FEED TANK (DA TANK):** A unit in the steam-water cycle used to (1) free the condensate of dissolved oxygen, (2) heat the feed water, and (3) act as a reservoir for feed water.

**DEBALLASTING:** The process of emptying salt from tanks, to protect the ship from underwater damage and increase its stability.

**DEGREE OF SUPERHEAT:** The amount by which the temperature of steam exceeds saturation temperature.

**DIATOMACEOUS EARTH:** A light, crumbly silica material derived from algae and microscopic skeletons. It has relatively high absorption and filtering qualities.

**DIATOMITE FILTERS:** Filters made of a diatomaceous earth and asbestos filler.

**DIRECT CURRENT (D-C):** Current that moves in one direction only.

**DIRECT DRIVE:** One in which the drive mechanism is coupled directly to the driven member.

**DISTILLATE:** Fresh water produced in distilling plants.

DISTILLING PLANTS: Units commonly called evaporators (evaps) used to convert seawater into fresh water.

DRAWING: The plans used to show the fabrication and assembly details.

DRUM, STEAM: The large tank at the top of the boiler in which the steam collects.

DRUM, WATER: A tank at the bottom of a boiler; also called MUD DRUM.

DRY PIPE: A perforated pipe at the highest point in a steam drum to collect steam.

DUCTILITY: Property possessed by metals that allows them to be drawn or stretched.

ECONOMIZER: A heat transfer device on a boiler that uses the gases of combustion to preheat the feed water.

EDUCTOR: A jet type pump (no moving parts) used to empty flooded spaces.

EFFICIENCY: The ratio of the output to the input.

ELASTICITY: The ability of a material to return to its original size and shape.

ELECTRODE: A metallic rod (welding rod) used in electric welding that melts when current is passed through it.

ELECTROHYDRAULIC STEERING: A system having a motor-driven hydraulic pump that creates the force needed to actuate the rams to position the ship's rudder.

ELECTROLYSIS: A chemical action that takes place between unlike metals in systems using salt water.

ELECTROMOTIVE FORCE (EMF): A force that causes electrons to move through a closed circuit; expressed in volts.

ELEMENT: A substance which consists of chemically united atoms of one kind.

ENERGY: The capacity for doing work.

ENGINEER'S BELL BOOK: A legal record maintained by the throttle watch of all ordered main engine speed changes.

ENGINE ORDER TELEGRAPH: A device on the ship's bridge to give orders to the engine-room. Also called ANNUNCIATOR.

EPM (EQUIVALENTS PER MILLION): The number of equivalent parts of a substance per million parts of another substance. The word "equivalent" refers to the equivalent weight of a substance.

EXPANSION JOINT: A junction which allows for expansion and contraction.

FATIGUE: The tendency of a material to break under repeated strain.

FEED HEATER: A heat transfer device used to heat the feed water before it goes to the boiler.

FEED WATER: Fresh water, with the highest possible level of purity, made in EVAPORATORS for use in boilers.

FERROUS METAL: Metal with a high iron content.

FIREBOX: The section of a ship's boiler where fuel oil combustion takes place.

FIREMAIN: The salt water line that provides fire-fighting and flushing water throughout the ship.

FIRE TUBE BOILER: Boilers in which the gases of combustion pass through the tubes and heat the water surrounding them.

FLAREBACK: A backfire of flame and hot gases into a ship's fireroom from the firebox. Caused by a fuel oil explosion in the firebox.

FLASH POINT OF OIL: That temperature at which the oil vapor will flash into fire but the main body of the oil will not ignite.

FLEXIBLE I-BEAM: An I-shaped steel beam on which the forward end of a turbine is mounted; it allows for longitudinal expansion and contraction.

FLOOR PLATES: The removable deck plating of a fireroom or engineroom aboard ship.

FLUX: A chemical agent that retards oxidation of the surface, removes oxides already present, and aids fusion.

FORCE: Anything that tends to produce or modify motion.

FORCED DRAFT: A term used to describe air under pressure supplied to the burners in a ship's boiler.

FORCED DRAFT BLOWERS: Turbine-driven fans which supply air to the boiler furnace.

FORCED FEED LUBRICATION: A lubrication system that uses a pump to maintain a constant pressure.

FORGING: The forming of metal by heating and hammering.

FRESH WATER SYSTEM: A piping system which supplies fresh water throughout the ship.

FUEL OIL MICROMETER VALVE: A valve installed at the burner manifold, which is used to control the fuel oil pressure to the burners.

FUEL OIL SERVICE TANKS: Tanks from which the fuel oil service pumps take suction for discharging oil to the burners.

FUSE: A protective device that is designed to open a circuit if the current flow exceeds a predetermined value.

GAGE GLASS: A device for indicating the liquid level in a tank.

GAS-FREE: A term used to describe a space that has been tested and found safe for hot work (welding & cutting).

GEARED-TURBINE DRIVE: A turbine that drives a pump, generator, or other machinery through reduction gears.

GROUNDED PLUG: A three pronged electrical plug used for grounding portable tools to the ship's structure. It is a safety device which always must be checked prior to using portable tools.

HAGEVAP SOLUTION: A chemical compound used in distilling plants, to prevent the formation of scale.

HALIDE LEAK DETECTOR: A device that is used to locate leaks in refrigeration systems.

HANDHOLE: An opening that is large enough for the hand and arm to enter the boiler for making slight repairs, and for inspection.

HANDY BILLY: A small portable water pump.

HARDENING: The heating and rapid cooling (quenching) of metal to induce hardness.

HARDNESS: The ability of a material to resist penetration.

HEAT EXCHANGER: Any device that is designed to allow the transfer of heat from one fluid (liquid or gas) to another.

HYDROGEN: A highly explosive, light, invisible, non-poisonous gas used for underwater welding and cutting operations.

HYDROMETER: An instrument used for determining the specific gravity of liquids.

HYDROSTATIC TEST: A pressure test using water to detect leaks in a boiler or other closed systems.

IGNITION, COMPRESSION: Ignition where the heat generated by compression in an internal combustion engine ignites the fuel (as in a diesel engine).

IGNITION, SPARK: Ignition where the mixture of air and fuel in an internal combustion-engine is ignited by an electric spark (as in a gasoline engine).

IMPELLER: An encased, rotating element provided with vanes which draw in fluid at the center and expel it at a high velocity at the outer edge.

IMPULSE TURBINE: A turbine in which the major part of the driving force is received from the impulse of incoming steam.

INDIRECT DRIVE: A drive mechanism coupled to the driven member by gears or belts.

INERT: Inactive.

INJECTOR: A device which, by means of a jet of steam, forces water into the boiler, or as in the diesel engineforces fuel into the cylinders.

INSULATION: A material used to retard heat transfer.

JACKBOX: Receptacle, usually secured to a bulkhead, in which telephone jacks are mounted.

JOB ORDER: The order issued by a repair activity to its own subdivisions, to perform a repair job in response to a WORK REQUEST.

JUMPER: Any connecting pipe, hose, or wire, normally for use in emergencies aboard ship, used to bypass damaged sections of a pipe, a hose, or & wire. (See BYPASS.)

JURY RIG: Any temporary or makeshift device.

LABYRINTH PACKING: Rows of metallic strips or fins used to prevent steam leakage along the shaft or a turbine.

LAGGING: A protective and confining cover placed over insulating material.

LIGHT OFF: Start, literally; 'to start a fire in," as in "light off a boiler."

LOG BOOK: Any chronological record of events, such as an engineering watch log.

**LOG, ENGINEERING:** A legal record of important events and data concerning the machinery of a ship.

**LOG ROOM:** Engineer's office on board ship.

**LUBE OIL PURIFIER:** A unit that removes water and sediment from lubricating oil by centrifugal force.

**MACHINABILITY:** The term used to describe the ease with which a metal may be turned, planed, milled, or otherwise shaped.

**MAIN CONDENSER:** A heat exchanger which converts exhaust steam to feed water.

**MAIN DRAIN SYSTEM:** The system used for pumping bilges, consisting of pumps and associated piping.

**MAKEUP FEED:** Water of required purity intended for use in ship's boilers. It is the water needed to replace that lost in the steam cycle.

**MALLEABILITY:** That property of a material which enables it to be stamped, hammered, or rolled into thin sheets.

**MANIFOLD:** A fitting with numerous branches used to convey fluids between a large pipe and several smaller pipes.

**MECHANICAL ADVANTAGE (MA):** The advantage (leverage) gained by the use of such devices as a wheel to open a large valve, chain falls and block and tackle to lift heavy weights, and wrenches to tighten nuts on bolts.

**MECHANICAL CLEANING:** A method of cleaning the firesides of boilers by scraping and wire-brushing.

**MICROMHOS:** Electrical units used with salinity indicators for measuring the conductivity of water.

**MOTOR GENERATOR SET:** A machine which consists of a motor mechanically coupled to a generator and usually mounted on the same base.

**NAVY BOILER COMPOUND:** A powdered chemical mixture used in boiler water treatment to convert scale-forming salts into sludge.

**NAVY SPECIAL FUEL OIL (NSFO):** The name applied to the grade of fuel oil that the Navy uses in combatant ships.

**NIGHT ORDER BOOK:** A notebook containing standing and special instructions by the engineer officer to the night engineering officer of the watch.

**NITROGEN:** An inert gas which will not support life or combustion. Used in recoil systems and other spaces requiring an inert atmosphere.

**NONFERROUS METAL:** Metals that are composed primarily of some element or elements other than iron.

**OFFICER OF THE WATCH (OOW):** Officer on duty in the engineering spaces.

**OIL KING:** A petty officer who receives, transfers, discharges, and tests fuel oil and maintains fuel oil records.

**OIL POLLUTION ACTS:** The Oil Pollution Act of 1924 (as amended) and the Oil Pollution Act of 1961 prohibit the overboard discharge of oil and water containing oil in port, in any sea area within 50 miles of land, and in special prohibited zones.

**ORIFICE:** A small opening.

**OVERLOAD RELAY:** An electrical protective device which automatically trips when a circuit draws excessive current.

**OXIDATION:** The process of various elements and compounds combining with oxygen. The corrosion of metals is generally a form of oxidation; rust on iron, for example, is iron oxide or oxidation.

**PANT, PANTING:** A series of pulsations caused by minor, recurrent explosions in the firebox of a ship's boiler. Usually caused by a shortage of air.

**PERIPHERY:** The curved line which forms the boundary of a circle (circumference), ellipse, or similar figure.

**PITOMETER LOG:** Device for indicating speed of ship and distance traveled by measuring water pressure on a tube projected outside the ship's hull.

**PLASTICITY:** That property which enables a material to be excessively and permanently deformed without breaking.

**PNEUMERCATOR:** A type of manometer used for measuring the volume of liquid in tanks.

**PPM (PARTS PER MILLION):** A comparison of the number of parts of a substance in a million parts of another substance. Used to measure the salt content of water.

PREHEATING: The application of heat to the base metal prior to a welding or cutting operation.

PRIME MOVER: The source of motion as a turbine, automobile engine, etc.

PUNCHING TUBES: The name applied to the mechanical means of cleaning the interiors of boiler tubes.

RADIATION, HEAT: The process of emitting heat in the form of heat waves.

REACH RODS: A length of pipe or back stock used as an extension on valve stems.

REACTION TURBINE: A turbine in which the major part of the driving force is received from the reactive force of steam leaving the blading.

REDUCER: Any coupling or fitting which connects a large opening to a smaller pipe or hose.

REDUCING VALVES: Automatic valves which are used to provide a steady pressure lower than the supply pressure.

REDUCTION GEAR: A set of gears used to transmit the rotation of one shaft to another at a slower speed.

REEFER: A provision cargo ship or a refrigerated compartment. An authorized abbreviation for refrigerator.

REFRIGERANT 12 (R-12): A nonpoisonous gas that is used in air conditioning and refrigeration systems.

REGULATOR (GAS): An instrument used to control the flow of gases from compressed gas cylinders.

REMOTE OPERATING GEAR: Flexible cables attached to valve wheels which permit the valves to be operated from another compartment.

RISER: A vertical pipe leading off a larger one; e.g., fireman riser.

ROOT VALVE: A valve located where a branch line comes off the main line.

ROTARY SWITCH: An electrical switch which closes or opens the circuit by a rotating motion.

SAE: Society of Automotive Engineers.

SAFETY VALVES: An automatic, quick opening and closing valve which has a reseat-pressure lower than the lift pressure.

SALINOMETER: A hydrometer that measures the concentration of salt in a solution.

SATURATION PRESSURE: The pressure corresponding to the saturation temperature.

SATURATION TEMPERATURE: The temperature at which a liquid boils under a given pressure. For any given saturation temperature there is a corresponding saturation pressure.

SCALE: Undesirable deposit, mostly calcium sulfate, which forms in the tubes of boilers.

SENTINEL VALVES: Small relief valves used primarily as a warning device.

SHAFT ALLEY: The long compartment of a ship in which the propeller shafts revolve.

SKETCH: A rough drawing indicating major features of an object to be constructed.

SLIDING FEET: A mounting for turbines and boilers to allow for expansion and contraction.

SLUDGE: The sediment left in fuel oil tanks.

SOLID COUPLING: A device used to join two shafts rigidly.

SOOT BLOWER: A soot removal device using a steam jet to clean the firesides of a boiler.

SPECIFIC HEAT: The amount of heat required to raise the temperature of one gram of a substance $1^{\circ}C$. All substances are compared to water which has a specific heat of 1.

SPEED-LIMITING GOVERNOR: A device for limiting the rotational speed of a prime mover.

SPEED-REGULATING GOVERNOR: A device that maintains a constant speed on a piece of machinery that is operating under varying load conditions.

SPLIT PLANT: A method of operating propulsion plants so that they are divided into two or more separate and complete units.

SPRING BEARINGS: Bearings positioned at various intervals along a propulsion shaft to help keep it in alignment and support its weight.

SPRINKLING SYSTEM: An automatic watering system used for cooling and flooding magazines and cargo spaces in case of fire.

STATIC: A force exerted by reason of weight alone, related to bodies at rest or in balance.

STEAM LANCE: A device for using low pressure steam inside of boilers to remove soot and carbon from boiler tubes.

STEERING ENGINE: The machinery that turns the rudder.

STERN TUBE: A watertight enclosure for the propeller shaft.

STRAIN: The deformation or change in shape of a material resulting from the applied load.

STRENGTH: The ability of a material to resist strain.

STRESS: Force producing or tending to produce deformation of a metal.

STUFFING BOX: A device to prevent leakage between a moving and a fixed part in a steam engineering plant.

STUFFING TUBE: A packed tube making a watertight fitting through a bulkhead for a cable or small pipe.

SUMP: A container, compartment, or reservoir; used as a drain or receptacle for fluids.

SUPERHEATER: A unit in the boiler that drys the steam and raises its temperature.

SWASH PLATES: Metal plates in the lower part of the steam drum that prevent the surging of boiler water with the motion of the ship.

SWITCHBOARD: A panel or group of panels with automatic protective devices, used to distribute the electrical power throughout the ship.

TANK TOP: Top side of tank section or double bottom of a ship.

TDC (TOP DEAD CENTER): The position of a reciprocating piston at its uppermost point of travel.

TEMPERING: The heating and controlled cooling of a metal to produce the desired hardness.

THIEF SAMPLE: A sample of oil or water taken from a ship's tank for analysis.

THROTTLEMAN: Man in the engineroom who operates the throttles to control the main engines.

THRUST BEARING: A bearing designed to limit the end play and absorb the axial thrust of a shaft.

TO BLOW TUBES: A procedure, using steam, for removing soot and carbon from the tubes of steaming boilers.

TOP OFF: To fill up, as a ship tops off in fuel oil before leaving port.

TOUGHNESS: That property of a material which enables it to withstand shock, and to be deformed without breaking.

TRANSFORMER: An electrical device used to step up or step down an a-c voltage.

TRICK WHEEL: A steering wheel in the steering engineroom or emergency steering station of a ship.

TUBE EXPANDER: A tool used to expand replacement tubes into their seats in boiler drums and headers.

TURBINE: A multibladed rotor, driven by steam or hot gas.

TURBINE JACKING GEAR: A motor-driven gear arrangement used to slowly rotate idle propulsion shafts and turbines.

TURBINE STAGE: The term applied to one set of nozzles and the succeeding row or rows of moving blades.

UPTAKES (EXHAUST TRUNKS): Large enclosed passages for exhaust gases from boilers to the stacks.

VENT: A valve in a tank or compartment used primarily to permit air to escape.

VENTURI INJECTOR: A device used for washing the firesides of boilers.

VOID: A small empty compartment below decks.

VOLATILE: The term used to describe a liquid that vaporizes quickly.

VOLTAGE TESTER (WIGGINS): A portable instrument that is used to detect electricity.

WATER TUBE BOILER: Boilers in which the water flows through the tubes and is heated by the gases of combustion.

WATER WASHING: A method of cleaning the firesides of boilers to remove soot and carbon.

WELDING LEAD: The conductor through which the electrical current is transmitted from the power source to the electrode holder and welding rod.

WHELPS: Any of the ribs or ridges on the barrel of a capstan or windlass.

WIREWAYS: Passageways, between decks and on the overheads of compartments, that contain electric cables.

WORK REQUEST: Request issued to a naval shipyard, tender, or repair ship for repairs.

ZERK FITTING: A small fitting to which a grease gun can be applied to force lubricating grease into bearings or moving parts of machinery.

ZINC: A metal placed in salt water systems to counteract the effects of electrolysis.

www.ingramcontent.com/pod-product-compliance
Lightning Source LLC
Chambersburg PA
CBHW081828300426
44116CB00014B/2507